In Our Own Words:
Writing From Parchman Prison

IN OUR OWN WORDS: WRITING FROM PARCHMAN PRISON

13#ISBN 978-0-9801944-0-1 10#ISBN 0-9801944-0-7
Published by VOX PRESS

Editor: Louis Bourgeois

Associate editors:
David Shirley
Simone Bourgeois
Patti Wrenn
Golda Ellington McLellan
Suanne Strider

Lay-out editor: Meg McConnell

All photos by Nate Murphree

Major sponsors of the Prison Writes Initiative include The Mississippi Humanities Council, Neil White, Carol Dorsey, The Cox Foundation, and The R&B Feder Foundation.

The Prison Writes Initiative would like to thank the Mississippi Department of Corrections for its support of the program.

PRAISE FOR IN OUR OWN WORDS: WRITING FROM PARCHMAN PRISON

Louis Bourgeois invited his Parchman students to write about their lives, their memories, how they saw the world as children, and how they grew as men. I am so grateful Louis made that invitation and that the men in his class responded with these beautiful, sad, observant, and richly described Delta stories. Gratitude to these writers for doing such hard and fine work, and gratitude to *In Our Own Words: Writing From Parchman Prison* for bringing these stories to us readers.

Judith Tannenbaum, author of *Disguised as a Poem: My Years Teaching Poetry at San Quentin* and other books

Riding on the back of a pet pig. Watching a baby being born in a cotton field. Outliving a hurricane before finishing grade school. Greeting mother from the backseat of a police car. These childhood memories will make you marvel not only because of their uniqueness but also because the stories could be yours or mine. But they are not just anyone's. They are the free expressions of inmates in the first Prison Writing Program at the Mississippi State Penitentiary at Parchman.

Grace Fisher. Communications Director for the Mississippi Department of Corrections

As you know, disparities in prisons are a huge issue. There is almost zero rehabilitation happening. My friend has an amazing program that helps prisoners in Parchman Prison. Louis Bourgeois (MFA), an accomplished editor and writer in his own right, has managed to pull off an amazing and perhaps legendary writing class at Parchman. He uses autobiography and philosophy as a means of teaching literacy and self-awareness.

I urge you to buy this book and support a much needed, nay necessary, humanities program.

Chris Aloia, MPH, Public Health Consultant for the University of Mississippi

As educators, we want to inspire, teach, and promote a positive change. Professor Bourgeois has magnificently taught his students to provide us an unfiltered glimpse into the lives of these men. All human beings, in prison or not, want to share their thoughts, ideas and experiences.

Nate Murphree, Academic Instructor at the Mississippi State Penitentiary

Prison Writes Initiative

A VOX PRESS PROGRAM

VOX
PRESS

TABLE OF CONTENTS

TABLE OF CONTENTS

Editor's Note

The book you are now holding in your hands is the result of an intense writing class conducted at Parchman Prison from January to June, 2014. The class, the first of its kind at Parchman, Mississippi's oldest and largest penitentiary, was spearheaded under VOX's new Prison Writes Initiative. Your purchase of the book, is a small but important step in allowing the program to expand ultimately into all of Mississippi's prisons. About the writing itself, I can only say this: men who had never written before in their lives, ended up churning out 10-40 page narratives, at an amazing speed and quality. I will let the book speak for itself. It is truly an amazing body of work and am very proud that I was involved in the process.

— Louis Bourgeois
   Coordinator and Instructor for the Prison Writes Initiative
   November, 2014

SERIEHEL BELTON
#33571

Seriehel Belton was born in Hazlehurst, Mississippi on December 27, 1978. He grew up in extreme poverty in the rural countryside of south Mississippi. He dropped out of school in the 6th grade. He is currently serving a thirty year sentence for cocaine distribution,

My Most Memorable Childhood Memories

Seriehel Belton

I was four or five years old when I had one of my most memorable childhood memories. I was attending my first school classes at the Children's Head Start Center in Hazlehurst, Mississippi. My mother was a teacher there, along with two other teachers, Ms. Virgil and Ms. Bogan. I felt privileged that my mother was my teacher.

My days at the Center weren't always as glowing as I could hope for, however. I recall having my first girlfriend there. I thought I was an amazing piece of work until I was caught in action getting my first kiss from my new girlfriend. I'd no idea what to say about it, nor could I even create a lie to tell my mother, or my teachers, that would be good enough to escape what I knew was sure to come. I did know that my only option to avoid a severe punishment was for me to be on my best behavior. That included doing all of my daily chores without being reminded or told to do them. That was my best way to not be punished. I went for it!

As soon as I came home from school, I changed out of my good school clothes and shoes and began to practice reciting my numbers. I fell sleepy after a bit of that, but before I went to sleep I was sure to take my bath and brush my teeth. With the first day of worrying behind me, and with many countless days to go, I knew that I had to make my mother proud of me in everything I did. Only with that achieved could I hope to avert my punishment. I knew that it would be harsh, because I'd been raised to not ever bring embarrassment to my mom, especially not to do so in public. With that in mind, my goal was to be the best student at the Learning Center. As well as my mother, I knew that I had to find favor with my other two teachers, Ms. Virgil and Ms. Bogan, in hopes that they would tell my mother how good I'd been. I needed all the help I could get.

Every day was a worry for me. I was even praying to God to save me from the expected severe whipping I was due. The only problem I had with praying was that I didn't know my bedtime prayers. I only knew how to say Grace, so I said Grace in place of any other prayers, hoping that God would understand and help me out.

Nearly five days had passed, which seemed like forever to me, and I'd started to think that maybe my consistent good behavior had caused my mother to forget about the whipping that she'd promised me. As the days went by I relaxed more and more. Maybe she really had forgotten or forgave me since I'd been so good for a whole week, so I eased back into my usual self at home and in school. That came quite easy for me, not to mention that it was fun too. However, after just a single day of being my old self at school my mother calmly reminded me on the way home that, "You were very grownup today. Even still, you know that I still owe you a whipping for last week, don't you?" That sank my heart and dashed all my hopes, so all I could do now was wait for my punishment and hope that I lived through it. I was ready for it when we arrived at our house. I went inside, changed out of my school clothes, and studied my color words until I got thirsty. I decided to ask for some soda. I was on my way with it back to my room when I fell down, spilling the soda all over my clothes, the carpet, and everything else. It was just my bad luck.

Immediately my mother came to the scene in a fiery rage, questioning me about how it happened. I tried to explain to her that it was a mistake and that I fell. She responded immediately, saying, "Didn't I tell you not to eat or drink in your room?!" All I could do was shake my head no, and then came the whipping that I'd dreaded for days. It seemed like it would never end. I must've said I'm sorry a hundred times, but finally it came to a stop. Just minutes later I realized that my nightmare was over.

II.

I was sitting in my room and staring out the window of the old shack that was the home for me and my single mother, and my sister and two brothers. Thoughts of Christmas loomed in my young mind as I replayed all the great stories and wishes that my school friends had shared with me, not to mention all the T.V. commercials with displays of new and sharp toys. I pictured joyful children with long Christmas gift lists. I was only nine years old, but I could clearly understand that the Christmas season was upon us and that Christmas was definitely on the horizon and approaching fast. However, the old rickety wooden shack that was our home bore not the first sign of Christmas or even the spirit of Christmas. In fact, the winter of the Christmas season brought only hardship to us in our poor living conditions. The constant and cold downpours of rain guaranteed us the extra responsibilities of trying to cover our second hand furniture in plastic to protect it from the water coming through our leaky roof. It always seemed that our supply of plastic covers and water buckets was never enough. With every rain that came it seemed that more and more of it came through our roof and windows. Every freeze brought the added stress of trying to find the supplies and ways to repair the pipes that burst with the freezing temperatures. We couldn't afford to call a handyman, no matter how cheap or reasonable his rates might have been. That left me and my two brothers the responsibilities and opportunities of being the repair men. We were compelled by necessity to learn things that we'd rather not learn, and then to make the repairs to the best of our abilities. We were of a young age, too young really, to shoulder these burdens, but I believe that we did our best.

The days until Christmas dwindled on our calendar, but brought no signs of it to our home. I listened closely to my mother, hoping to hear some indication that our Christmas would come, but not a word was spoken from her about it. I'd test the waters by a casual mention of Christmas and she'd respond by saying, "Son, be thankful that we're able to have food on the table." That was far from what I was hoping to hear.

With Christmas only days away, I didn't want to believe that our house would be without it, especially after hearing the wonderful things about it from my school friends and seeing it on our T.V. So in my mind, I came up with the idea that it was going to be a surprise! I told my sister this, and both my brothers too. They agreed, thinking the same thoughts. We all hoped that Christmas would come to our house. I figured that besides the gifts, something else was also missing. The food! There were no signs of preparation for the cakes, pies, turkey and ham that usually filled the table on Christmas. I didn't mention that thought to my three siblings. I kept that to myself. As badly as I hated to think about Christmas, and how happy every other kid was about it, I just couldn't bear the thought anymore. I decided to go to my mother and ask her, "Mom, are we going to have a Christmas and get any presents?" It was a big question to ask of her, and it paralyzed her. She sat still for a moment on the side of her bed, looking straight ahead in a daze. I sat next her waiting for an answer. It seemed like forever had passed and I thought that maybe she hadn't heard me. And then, with tears rolling form her eyes she said, "Son, we're just not able to have a Christmas." At that very moment my fate was sealed and final.

III.

The summer of '86 was quickly approaching while the heavy and hurtful thoughts of our hopeless Christmas receded into the far corners of my mind. The summer on the horizon showed no signs of financial stability for us. I could only see a revolving cycle of broken dreams and unrealized hopes. These were my thoughts as I looked out the window of our shack in the woods of Hazlehurst, Mississippi. My sister and brothers, and my single mother and I called it home.

I can vividly remember my mother saying, "Someday things will get better." That's now, but back then in my young mind I was thinking that she always says this, but things never seemed to get better. They only seemed to get worse.

As my mother worked faithfully at her job in a convalescent home, I knew even as a kid that her duties at work weren't an easy task. She'd tell us stories about how she coped with the unfairness of her co-workers and the staff. We didn't have a vehicle at the time, so my mother would have to get to and from work the best way she could. I feel that was probably more of a task than the job itself. Sometimes my aunt would pick her up from work with the nastiest attitude, rushing her off as if she was a child. Even though I was very young it angered me, almost as much as when my mother would have to walk home from work in the blistering summer heat after a long day of work. This cycle of despair seemed to be a never ending process made to destroy us.

These memories, and more, are the most memorable ones of my childhood.

13

Hard Childhood

Serhiel Belton

Back we'd go to the old and cold dim shack that was our home.

I'd grown accustomed to the hardships that life sent my way in my young life. The only thing that ever seemed to change, were the days of the week and the dates on the calendar, but even with those changes the hardships never seemed to relent.

With the summer of '86 finely tuned and strongly in effect, our small family would always hope for better days. All the while, we wondered in our hearts if it was even possible for us to have a better life. Being that it was summer and school was out, my mother still worked at the local convalescence home. She faced the same daily struggles that she had for so long endured.

My sister would always stay at our grandmother's house, being that she was the only girl and the youngest of the family. My grandmother's house was the ideal place for her to be. All of us wished that our living conditions could be, and someday would be, like hers.

Her house was a cozy, average sized house made of brick. It was located close to the center of town and in a nice, quiet neighborhood with friendly neighbors and beautifully landscaped lawns.

We'd usually visit grandmother's house on various weekends, and it was always a highlight for us. We knew we'd have a breakfast served to us promptly in the morning. That was definitely not the norm for us.

Before we ate breakfast, our grandmother would tell us to go wash our hands. We'd come to the table to say Grace, and our plates would be there already. She would fill each one equally with bacon and eggs, biscuits and jelly, and a helping of oatmeal to round it off.

It was almost unbelievable how excited we were at even the thought of such a good meal. We'd quickly empty our plates and ask for more, which would send Grandma back to the kitchen where she'd be scraping and raking the boilers, pots and pans until everything was completely gone. Sometimes she'd say that we ate like starved horses, but little did she know how close to the truth she was. We wouldn't get a good, hot meal like that again until our next visit to her house, and we were starved.

After breakfast we'd watch the newest cartoons that came on her cable T.V., which was another plus for visiting Grandma's house. At our house we only had the basic channels with no cable. Our old box television set would fry so hard until we'd have to wrestle with the station endlessly, trying to get the picture to show. Without that, most of the time we could hear the T.V. show, but we couldn't see it. By the time we got it to clear up a little, the show would be off, or close to being off. Grandma's house had an abundance of luxuries for us to be excited about.

After the cartoons were over, we'd be let out to play. Grandma would say, "Stay in the yard and stay away from that road!" We'd play kick-ball with the neighbors' kids, and then we'd foot-race a lot, but those kids didn't like playing with us, because they said that we'd play too rough with them. We'd play endlessly, despite the sweltering summer heat which never bothered us much, but to our grandma it was a constant concern. She would check on us as we played in the yard, always reminding us not to get too hot. We'd respond to her concerns by saying, "Yes ma'am, we're okay." Her pleas went in one ear and out the other immediately, and our playing would continue until we'd take a break for water. We knew that she'd have several pitchers of different flavors of Kool-Aid waiting for us to drink.

To me and my two brothers, this was how the children on T.V. lived. We weren't use to anything like this at home. Back there at our shack we hardly had running water, much less anything like Kool-Aid to drink. After our break, we'd get right back to our play.

We weren't use to playing with real toys and up-to-date gadgets. All our toys were home-made from sticks, bricks, rocks, and old bicycle rims and parts.

Our grandma would then call us in for lunch, which at her house was always ready at 12 p.m. sharp. She'd call us in and instruct us in the same routine of washing our hands before coming to the table to say Grace before we ate. That was never a problem for us, because we were so excited to receive another hot, full-course meal.

After supper we'd go back outside to sit on the front porch, watching the cars drive by. Back home, we lived so far out in the woods we didn't see any cars at all. We didn't have a car of our own, so watching them go by grandma's house was quite amusing for a small family that didn't have anything.

We were happy to get a good warm bath without having to heat the water on the stove in pots and pans, and then tote them to the bathroom. That was our daily routine at home. Clean clothes were another luxury.

Grandma's house was surely the closest thing to Heaven for us. Nothing was better than being with her at her house.

It was late afternoon when we all had a bath. After that, we'd no longer be allowed outside, under no- circumstances. Dinner would be on the horizon and served exactly at 5 p.m. We knew the routine - wash our hands and say Grace.

My brothers and I knew that dinner was the sign that our day in paradise was almost over. Shortly we'd be back in the dreadful clutches of what we called home.

As time rolled by, my brothers and I would know soon that our mother would be arriving from work with my aunt or whoever else would be able to give her a ride. Most of the time it would be my aunt, who drove her to grandma's house to pick us up.

Grandma would go to the door when she pulled up, calling out, "Ya'll mom done made it to pick ya'll up." Our hearts would sink from the thought of what was to come. Back we'd go to the old and cold dim shack that was our home. We'd file out the front door, faces sad and heads hung low, hugging Grandma good bye. We'd pile into my aunt's car where she and my mom would be waiting for us. We'd sit in the back of my aunt's 1986 steel-gray Taurus. My aunt would make us all put on our seatbelts. Of course we weren't use to riding in a nice vehicle, much less fastening our seatbelts. That was something that people did on T.V. and in the movies. We had never owned a car.

We'd all wave bye to Grandma as we drove away, and we would continue to wave until we couldn't see her anymore. Our aunt's new car would quickly move to the nearest intersection, and we'd all become silent as we gradually left the city and headed toward the rural county of Hazelhurst. Soon we'd be turning down a rocky road that led to our rock-filled drive way. We knew we were surely at home as we came closer and closer to our beat-up and color-faded shack. Finally we came to a stop before it. "We're here," said my older brother, Russell. My mother got out first, and we'd all file out of the back seat, one by one, closing the car door behind us. She'd quickly pull away, in a hurry to reach her next destination.

The door to our shack was secured with a string, and my mother had to untie it before we could go inside to our dreadful house. We were welcomed by the pungent and unpleasant odor of old, rotten, wet and mildewed wood that came from the rainwater that entered through the walls and roof. Our adventure to Grandma's house was over, and we were home again.

It was our routine to scramble and find the kitchen matches, so we could light our kerosene lamps that we used for light. We had three of them, one in the kitchen, one in the front room as you entered the door, and one that we'd rotate from the bathroom to the room that all of us slept in. Because it rained through the walls and windows, we couldn't use electricity, which we couldn't afford anyway.

That's the reason my mother had the electricity turned off, and when we children asked why, she explained to us that she didn't want any of us to get electrocuted by the morning rain. In some parts of the house, we looked up and could see holes as big as plates from where the roof had sunk in, and we could see gaping holes in the bathroom and kitchen walls.

We'd put cardboard over them as covers, but insects and other critters would somehow find their way through our cardboard barricades. We'd always see big lizards running up the walls, along with the rats, but for us, that was the usual and quite common.

For our family, life offered no guarantees and definitely no promises. It was about surviving one day to the next. This way of life had become so common for us that it was the only thing we expected. We figured that if we could simply manage to have enough to eat each day, then that was a good day for us. My mother received food stamps from the W.I.C. program, which was a government program that gave low income families free cheese, bread, powdered eggs and milk at the beginning of each month, and for us, that was more exciting than Christmas, because we knew at least we'd have something to eat. The food didn't last for very long, but my mother would teach us not to eat it all in one sitting. However, what she said would often fall on deaf ears. We were so happy to receive the W.I.C. food that we would eat all that we could, and that would make my mother angry sometimes. She didn't understand that we weren't use to having that much food. We felt we were starving, and we always hoped and wished for a good meal. She'd tell us that our food issue had to last us through the month, but we being kids didn't know the value of anything. All we knew is that we were hungry.

We were only use to eating some homemade food that we made for ourselves, like mustard sandwiches, syrup sandwiches, mayonnaise sandwiches, and sometimes just straight bread-on-bread sandwiches. The problem with sandwiches was that the rats would get to the bread and eat holes out of it and the ends off of it, but we couldn't throw the bread away, because that was all we had. So we'd break off all the parts that the rats ate, and we'd eat the rest.

Our food supply was further challenged by our lack of a refrigerator. When my mother would get her food stamps and go grocery shopping, the meats she bought would be taken to my grandmother's house to be stored there. Even so, by the middle of the month, everything would be gone and we'd be right back to square one.

The summer of '86 was ending, and the start of school was approaching, and the thought of what I had to face weighed heavily on my mind. I had not the things I needed - backpack, shoes, clothes, or even a new haircut. I felt that I wouldn't have many friends, if any at all, so I focused on what I'd do. I really wanted to find a way to quit school, because I didn't have what I needed to fit in, and I knew that the other kids would make fun of me and talk about me. My shoes were old and busted around the sides. My clothes were ill-fitting, and anyone could see that they were hand-me-downs, which they were.

The only reason that I did want to go to school was that I knew I'd get a chance to eat a good lunch and breakfast, but with all the kids making fun of me, and talking about me, I didn't know if it would be worth it. The food was the only thing about school that was appealing to me, and it's sad to me that I could only think about having a good meal. But that's exactly how it was in 1986 for me and my family.

Broken

Seriehel Belton

As the years steadily changed, the desire to live beyond poverty remained branded in my heart and mind. By any means, I was open for almost anything that would bring us out of poverty. I was only waiting for the moment and the opportunity to present itself. I had no idea what that opportunity might be, but at that point in time in my life, it didn't really matter to me what it was. I was like a sinner in the lowest depths of fiery Hell thirsting for a drink of water. The level of our poverty was taking its toll on my mom. It began to show in her actions and appearance, robbing her little by little of her sanity. When we'd do things that deserved punishment, our punishment would be so severe and unfair to the point that all I could think was that either our mother was going crazy or had simply got to the point that she hated her own children. Some of those methods of punishment changed my life forever, hardening my heart and leaving me to wonder, "Lord why are you letting this happen to us?" Sometimes my mother would come home from work and wouldn't speak to us. We hardly ever knew what to think of her mood swings, but always we knew they weren't ever good at all, for her and for us. We were at the point of being afraid of our mother. Sometimes, being children, we forgot to do some of our chores, like taking out the trash, or washing the dishes, or picking up branches and sticks out of the yard. Our mother would wait until we were asleep at night, and then come in and wake us up by lashing us with an electrical extension cord, striking us with it wherever she could, our face, our backs, our arms and legs, etc. That left humiliating and embarrassing welts and marks on our young bodies, because the cord was doubled up in her hand to shorten it for efficiency. It would leave long, heavy and deep marks wherever it struck us. After this harsh and random beating by the cord, she'd make us get out of all our clothes so she could whip us one by one. When she was finished with that she ordered us outside to stand naked in the winter-cold air of our back yard. Often there would be drizzling rain with light snow on the ground. She'd yell at us, "You better not leave that spot or knock on the door!" We'd stay outside naked in the blistering cold rain for an hour or more. I'd be so cold that I couldn't hardly move. I'd try to say something to my brothers, but I was so cold that I could hardly speak. We'd try to hug each other, so we wouldn't be so cold, but nothing seemed to warm us up. We had a small dog that would always come running up to us; which made us grateful because we'd take turns holding that fluffy and warm little dog to help us warm up even a bit. It seemed to us like we stood there for eternity. We would talk to God and ask Him to please let us be able to go back inside, because we didn't want to freeze to death. Sometimes our mother would come to the door, and if we weren't standing in the same spot that she told us to, she'd close the door and make us stay naked in the cold even longer. When we were finally allowed to come back inside, we'd be so cold that we could barely walk to the door to get back inside. We had to help each other make steps to the house. We'd be so glad to get back to our shack. Once inside, it seemed to be impossible to warm up, but despite that, our mom would still make us do our chores. I knew our mom loved us, but that didn't help me understand why she would treat us this way. After we finished the chores we'd forgotten to do, we went straight to bed to be ready for school in the morning.

VINCENT YOUNG
#37525

Vincent young was raised on a farm in New Albany, Mississippi. His father was an airplane mechanic and sometimes bare knuckles boxer. He is serving a life sentence for armed-robbery and aggravated assault.

I. The Pet

Vincent Young

New Albany, Mississippi
Out in the country - 1968

I'm six years old. My sister and I are playing outside, chasing each other around and through the pine trees by our home. Our mother is on the porch shelling peas and watching us play. "Truck" - our pet hog - suddenly appears. We call her "Truck" because she's so long.

Truck joins in our play by chasing us around and through the pine trees. She was so long that we'd take turns riding around on her back. Mother called out, "You kids might be in trouble when your daddy comes home!" That's because he'd always tell us to let Truck out of her pen before we began to play. Otherwise, she would be so excited to join us that she'd break out of the pen and chase us around.

We forgot to let her out that morning, and sure enough she broke out. My sister and mother and I went to fix it, but first we had to round up the other hogs and return them to the pen. We tried to fix the fence before daddy came home, but all we did was make it worse. When he did come home he surprised us all by not being angry. He did nothing but laugh, and we laughed too.

Daddy went to fix the fence, but first we had to count the hogs to know that none were missing.

They were all there safely inside the repaired fence when we were through, and the next day we did exactly what daddy told us. We let Truck out first, before our play began, and the fence was fine when we were done.

That day we went to pick berries, my sister, mother, and me. And Truck. She ate more berries than we could pick. Truck really loved her berries.

Everyone else had the usual cats and dogs, but we had a pig who was part of the family. When Truck was little she stayed in the house, but we had to keep her outside when she got big. She was so big that when she did come into the house she'd always knock things over.

We had a lot of fun when it was time to give her a bath. It was easy when she was little. We'd just put her in a bucket. When she got big it was like washing a car. It seemed that every time we got her clean, she'd go and wallow in the mud! Then my sister and I would have to wash her again! It took two baths to keep her clean for the day.

A few months later Truck died. She wouldn't get up and come to me when I went to feed her one morning. Even when I went into the pen she still wouldn't get up. I ran to daddy to tell him and he told me when we got there that Truck was dead. I cried so long I thought I'd never stop. I continued my weeping when daddy gave Truck a funeral. He built a coffin for Truck which we placed in the grave that he'd dug himself. I was surprised when so many people came to Truck's funeral, including all my uncles, aunts, cousins, and friends. Daddy said some words over her grave. It was a proper and moving ceremony.

My sister and I were sad for a while, until daddy brought us another pig. This one we named "Legs" because her legs were so long. My sister and I took turns feeding her from a bottle and taking her outside to go potty. All our fun started anew with Legs.

Daddy made Legs a special pen in the barn, which made more work to keep it clean for my sister and I. We didn't mind, because we didn't want Legs to go the way of Truck.

She'd stay in our room some nights after she was house-broken, and mommy didn't minds as long as we kept her clean. Still, we never forgot Truck because she was our first pet.

I still wonder to this day how we chose to have a pig for a pet instead of a dog. Daddy had plenty of dogs, mostly hunting dogs. Maybe pigs made a good pet for us because we could ride them when they got big and you can't ride a dog like that.

II. Cotton Picking

Vincent Young

The time I'd liked least as a six year old was cotton picking time. That season came around about late September and October. My sister and I had to go out to the cotton field every morning with our mother. You may wonder why a six year old is in a field every morning instead of school, but that was normal in 1968. My parents didn't trust the school with kids as young as us, so we had to wait until we were nine. Until then we were homeschooled by our mother.

My mother would give us a pillow case to put our cotton in. The mornings would be cool and the cotton would be wet from the dew. My fingers would get wet and cool. They'd get so cold they would hurt, but I never told my mother. She called me her "little man", and I was trying to be that little man for her.

My sister and I were the only kids out there working. Everyone else were adults, mostly women.

I always noticed how they were dressed, with big straw hats hanging on their back from a string around their necks. When the sun was low and the morning was cool, they'd put on their hats by 11 A.M., my mother too. We didn't have hats on a string around our neck, but my sister always wore a scarf to cover her head from the sun.

I'd fill up my pillow case about ten times a day, with most of it coming from the other women. They'd reach into my sack when my mother wasn't looking and fill it with some of their cotton.

My sister didn't pick much cotton, mostly she'd lay on my mother's long cotton sack and let her drag my sister down the rows.

I saw the women take off their shoes about noon when the dirt warmed up. My mother would give me a kiss every time I'd empty my pillow case into her sack, and I wanted my kisses from my mother because her kisses meant she loved me and I was doing good.

There was a lot of singing, from my mother mostly. She'd be asked to sing a church song, and she can really sing. Even the preachers in their churches would ask her to come sing, but she always told them no because she had two children to raise.

One day I saw a baby born in the field. The lady was putting some cotton in my pillow case and I noticed her feet getting wet, looking like she'd used the bathroom down her legs. Then she grabbed her stomach and started yelling. The other women close by came running and laid her down on her back, raising her dress and I could see everything. Between her legs was something coming out of her. I moved closer to get a better look and I saw a little head poking out. I don't know who hollered louder, me or the woman, and I cut a trail to my mother for help. The way this woman was yelling told me that whatever was coming out of her must be bad! I reached at my mother and told her what I saw. She explained to me that the woman was having a baby.

The day after the birth, my mother caught me getting cotton from the other women and she called me by my whole name. That's a sign I was in deep trouble. She made me work by her side for the rest of the day. I couldn't run around the field getting cotton from the other women. I only got four kisses that day instead of ten. Once we got home she told me to go to the kitchen table and that meant I was going to receive a talking to about what I'd done. When I got there she got on me for taking cotton from the other women. She told me that those women gave me cotton because they thought we were poor after seeing my sister and I in the fields instead of in school.

My time to go to school was almost here, so it was a short year in the fields for me when I was around seven years old. I'd always wanted to go but now that my time was near I wasn't so sure. My uncertainty arose when I'd heard some stories about it. I'd never seen a white kid my age.

We didn't go to town to shop. The town came to us in the back of a truck called a rolling store. You name it and it was there, shoes, jeans, bread, milk, lumber, nails, power saws, dressers, car tires, bikes, meat, flour, and candy. So we had no need to go to town, and that's why I'd never seen a white kid my age. I'd heard many stories about them, especially about their behavior. I lived in dread of turning nine years old because I loved the world I was in. Everyone was black and seemed to be friends. There were twenty-one houses around each other and no more than ½ mile apart. All I've seen was my race of people, including the driver of the rolling store. I've seen white men on T.V. Sometimes a white man would come into our area selling stuff, but they never stayed long because one of the men would tell them, "No one here is buying anything today." They told him that every time, but he always returned the next month. I was thinking too far ahead of myself because I still had two more years of running in the fields and playing with Legs.

III. First Encounter With Racism in 1969, in the Small Town of New Albany, Mississippi

Vincent Young

I went to a sale barn with my daddy when I was seven years old. A sale barn is a place where you buy and sell livestock. My daddy and I went there to sell fifteen of our forty hogs. We were sitting in a small arena that held about 150 people. The animals were brought out as a showcase and a white man began calling out numbers so fast that I couldn't keep up. All the white men sat on one side and the few black men there were on the other side. A black kid was bringing the animals in and out. My daddy always brought me things, but this was our first time out together. I'd gone hunting with him, but this was different, because I'd never been with him to a place outside of our world before.

This was a new experience for me. The first thing I noticed about the white men was that all of them were spitting black-looking stuff out of their mouths. The way they talked was strange, as well. The words that stuck in my mind were, "By God!" and "Nigger". I knew about "By God!" but I didn't know what "Nigger" meant. All I know was that a white man said to me, "By God, Nigger! What're you looking at me for?!" I was looking at him because he had the biggest booger hanging out his nose that I'd ever seen and I looked at it in a trance with my mouth wide open. I could hear him, but I was speechless. The man turned away, mumbling something, and just then daddy gave me a dollar to buy myself a hamburger and a Coca-Cola.

I left the sale barn and walked 100 paces to the place they sold the food. I noticed white people looking at me there, and I thought that was because the bell rang on the door when I opened it. At the counter I asked the man for a hamburger and coke, but I had to ask him again because he didn't seem to hear me even though I showed him the dollar bill. He said, "Boy, can't you read?" When I said yes he grabbed my arm, took me outside, and told me to read the sign which said, *Coloreds Served around Back.* The white man gave me a crazy look and went back inside. A black man who was standing outside and saw this happen showed me the way around to the back. We had to go by all the horses, cows, hogs and goats to get to the back window which had a pen on each side of it. One pen held cows and the other held goats, and both of them were bad-smelling. Around those two pens were about 100 more, with half of them being filled with more animals.

When I got back to daddy, I told him what'd happened. He said he was sorry that he hadn't explained to me about black and white people. I asked him, "What are coloreds and niggers?" He explained to me that the words had different meanings. Colors mean red, yellow, orange, green, and so on, but some dumb man had made the word colors include our skin color.

Daddy also told me about the word, nigger, saying that it's a disgrace word, and a word made up to break the spirit of our race. He told me, "Never let anyone call you a nigger

27

and get away with it." He asked me who called me a nigger, and I showed him the man who did it. I watched daddy give all his money and his truck keys to his friend before he told me to come with him. He led me over to that white man and told him to apologize to me for calling me a nigger. The man turned very red and said, "I didn't know that was your boy, L.D." See, L.D. is my daddy's initials from when he used to box bare knuckles to skull on the weekends, which is boxing without gloves on. The white man apologized to me and gave me a dollar, so I went and bought my sister a burger and a coke too, and with the leftover change from both dollars I was able to buy Legs a burger too. Daddy asked, "Who're the extra burgers for?" I told him, "for Mattie and Legs." He said, "Legs eats better than any pig I've ever seen!"

That day changed the way I looked at the world, because now I knew the world looked differently at me. I did my best to explain what happened to Mattie, but I had a bad stutter which caused her to run to mommy and daddy.

A few weeks later we all gathered around the kitchen table, and that's when I learned that the white race called us "colored" or "nigger". My mother and father told my sister Mattie and I that our blood-line comes from Africa, making us Africans. So no matter what anyone else says, I know I'm somebody. I'm not a nigger or a colored person. I'm an African-American born in the U.S.A. I'm a man with strong roots and love for his family.

We had a T.V. in our home. Mattie and I were only allowed to watch certain shows like I Love Lucy, The Rifleman and cartoons. We weren't allowed to watch Tarzan because our parents felt it was too racist. Daddy felt that the show was saying that everything must be controlled by the white man, even the animals, and he didn't want us to watch shows like that.

IV. Flying 1969

Vincent Young

My daddy and I became closer after that day at the sale barn. He'd always taught me about fishing, hunting, and how to defend myself, and he even took me with him to his work sometimes. My father was an airplane mechanic at a nearby small airport. I didn't know that airplanes were so big. I'd never seen them up close, only in the air and on the T.V. Most of the day all I did was walk around and look at them, climbing up on them to look inside. They looked funny inside because the control panel had more monitors than a car's dashboard and the plane's steering wheel was only half of a car's wheel. Some had two seats and some had four. I soon found out that my father was a pilot and he knew how to fly the planes that he worked on. He asked me, "Do you want to fly with me?" I said, "Yes!" and "No!" at the same time. I knew I had to go with him because I wanted to know what it felt like to fly! I must tell you that I'd tried to fly, jumping off chairs while flapping my arms like wings, or jumping off the porch with a sheet tied around my neck. My most daring, and dangerous, attempts were made by running real fast and diving into the air, thinking that I'd take to the air and fly! All I ever got from my tests of flying were skinned knees, elbows, my chin, and a hurt pride. My father offered me the chance to really fly and I took it! He put me in the seat and buckled me up. I'll admit that I was a little scared, but I'd dreamed about flying and tried to so many times that I couldn't pass up the chance to do it for real. "I'm with my daddy so what could go wrong," I thought. Daddy started the engine which was very loud to me, and he yelled, "Here we go!"

I felt the plane turning, but he wasn't turning the wheel, only stepping on pedals that looked like brakes. We started moving down the runway very fast and when we were close to the end he pulled back on the wheel and off the ground we went! That rising motion made my stomach feel queasy, but once we leveled out I felt alright. At that moment I wanted to be a pilot like my father. He told me to look out the window, and when I did I could see for miles and miles. Everything on the ground looked so small to me. The sky was beautiful with the sun shining brightly. I saw cars on the roads that looked like ants, and houses that looked like play houses. I wanted to stay in the air forever.

The only discomfort I had was the take-off and the landing, with the landing most of all because then the plane would bounce. I found out why my father was a great airplane mechanic. It was because he was also the tester of his work. Every plane he worked on was flown by him first. "Who are you talking to?" I asked him. "That's the control tower, Vincent."

My legs felt funny when we were back on the ground, but I didn't care. I was ready to go back up! I couldn't wait to tell Mattie when we got back home. She didn't believe me, so daddy told her that she can go with him tomorrow. I couldn't sleep at all that night, like a kid on the night before Christmas. But you already know that you always fall asleep before Santa Claus comes to your house.

Daddy woke us up very early so we could be ready to go with him. As Mattie and I ate our breakfast we could hear Mommy fussing at our daddy. I couldn't make out what she was saying to him, but I knew it wasn't good. We left the house with daddy after we'd finished eating, and on the way to the airport he told us that today would be our last day going with him because mommy didn't like being home alone.

I showed Mattie the plane Daddy and I flew yesterday once we arrived at the airport, but then we took a different plane. This one was painted orange and white. We got into that one, and when we started down the runway my sister grabbed my hand and squeezed it tightly. I knew she was scared. I was too, my first time. Her holding my hand was her sign to me that she was afraid, but she was alright once we leveled off. Just like me she was amazed at how things looked from the air, how beautiful was the sky, and how bright was the sun.

Our daddy never took us to work with him again, and yet that didn't end my desire to fly. I did the next best thing. I built my own airplane. Daddy and Mattie gave me a lot of help, mostly daddy when he got off work early. Three weeks later we had our airplane! It was made of wood and big enough to ride in, only it had no motor, so we had to push it, making the airplane sound with our mouth which was okay. Daddy even had it painted orange and white, with three tires, two in the front and one in the back. My daddy can build most anything made out of wood. Mattie and I played airplane for many years to come.

V. 1970

Vincent Young

I've still got a year before I have to go to school. Home schooling is getting harder, especially reading out loud, because I still had a stuttering problem. My sister and I had our own sign language that we'd used for years because of my stuttering. When I'd get excited I'd stutter even worse. Certain words, like those that began with a "W", would be difficult to say.

One thing I did have was girlfriends, although I couldn't speak with them without stuttering. Because of that I said little to them. Maybe it was because I was the only kid in the area with an airplane.

Things weren't too good for me as an eight year old. I was always in a fight with someone over girls, or if they were mocking me. I always seemed to win. That's because my daddy taught me how to fight. I learned later, as I got older, that my daddy whipped a lot of the other daddies in the area. That might be why I had so many fights! Their sons wanted revenge because my daddy beat up their daddy. My daddy did teach me one other thing: never be afraid of anyone, and so I became pretty good at fighting.

The fights I got into were with much older boys. My sister would always try to play doctor and patch me up before going home because we both knew how Mommy would fuss at me.

One thing I can say is that I only got one whipping at home for fighting. I heard mommy and daddy talking about me that night, and after that night I never got another whipping for fighting. I saw my daddy fight only once. It was in our front yard. I remember the man was fresh from another fight because one of his eyes had a black ring around it. My sister and I were outside playing when Mr. Richard came walking fast into our yard and straight up onto the porch, where he knocked on the door. Daddy came outside and made us go into the house. Once inside we saw mommy looking out the window. I went to the window to see what she was looking at. By now, there were about ten people standing in our yard and looking at my daddy and Mr. Richard. I saw Mr. Richard take a swing at my daddy and miss. Daddy barely moved. He swung back, hitting Mr. Richard in the side of his neck. Mr. Richard stumbled, but kept his balance. Daddy let him regain his footing. I could see my daddy ready for action with both of his fists balled up. I was amazed at how light and swift my daddy was on his feet. Mr. Richard was only hitting my daddy's arms, because daddy was blocking most of his punches. All of a sudden Mr. Richard nailed my daddy a good one. The fight seemed to stop. I saw my daddy smiling. I didn't know why he was smiling, but MR. Richard began to back away with both his hands in the air as if to surrender. Daddy didn't accept that and advanced on Mr. Richard, hitting him so hard that we could hear the lick inside the house. Mr. Richard seemed to leave the ground, and the thought of flying crossed my mind. I looked around the yard for my airplane, but mommy brought my thoughts back to the fight by rapping on the window. Mr. Richard was laid out on the ground, not moving. The other men were patting my daddy on the back. The fight had only lasted a few minutes. Daddy threw five punches— one neck shot, two gut shots, one side shot, and the final upper cut. With that one the fight was over.

Mommy went outside, fussing at the other men to leave. They almost had to carry Mr. Richard, but before he left I saw him and daddy shake hands.

Mommy got on daddy for fighting in the front yard. She doctored on him like my sister did with me, sticking cotton up his nose and putting some type of meat right below his left eye. Now I see where my sister got her doctor ways.

I never saw my daddy fight again. I knew he was still fighting, because I'd see the cuts on his hands and a few on his face. I'd ask him, "Did you win?" He'd say, "Yes." I counted eighteen straight times, until one morning when he said, "No. I lost." I was unsure if that made me happy or sad. I felt somewhere in between the two, because I'd just lost a fight myself to a twelve year old, which was also my first loss. I've always heard the saying, "Like father, like son." That's just what happened to me and my daddy. I was sad and happy that he'd lost a fight, because I'd just lost a fight, and I wanted to be just like my daddy. After he'd told me about his loss I knew that I still had a chance to be like him.

Things changed for me after a few more fights because guys stopped picking on me, although we still fought over girls now and then.

The year was passing fast and soon I'd be starting school. I dreaded that the most. Kids older than me went to an all black school until 1969. I'd be one of the first in our family to go to a black and white school. I was so afraid of that day.

VI. First Day of School, September 1971, age 9 - Registration

Vincent Young

Kids older than me went to an all black school until 1969. I'd be one of the first in our family to go to a black and white school. I was so afraid of the day.

My mother was with me on the first day because she had to register me into school. The first thing I noticed was a white kid, around my age, running down the hall, which was so long like a row of cotton, and it looked wet but it wasn't. We went into this room that had a lot of people there already. Everyone in this room was black, except the four white women sitting behind a long table. Mommy took me to one of these women who asked my mommy a bunch of questions about me. The only question I recall was why I wasn't registered already years ago. That started words between her and mommy about me not being in school last year. I could tell mommy was upset by the way she ran her hand over her face. I heard her say, "No one is going to tell me how to raise my children?" We started to leave but were stopped by another woman at the same table, so I got to register that day.

We left and walked back down the same hall. I noticed each room that we passed had a bunch of funny looking chairs in them. We also met a few white kids with their mothers, and they would always get as far away from us as they could. The little white kids and I would just stare at each other.

I had a thousand questions for daddy and mommy on the ride back home, but I had to tell my sister through sign language, so she could say my questions to them. I thought, "How will I make it through school next week without her?" My questions were mostly about the little white kids. Will I be in the same room with them? Can Mattie come with me? Daddy told me that she could go with me next year, but this year I'd have to go by myself.

Going to my first day of school was made into a special event at our house. I got ice cream, cookies, and soda-pop. Mommy baked a cake and cooked my favorite meal: chicken, rice, biscuits and gravy. I made sure my sister got everything that I got to eat and drink. There were five days before I was to start school, and those were the fastest five days of my life. On the last night I went to sleep, and the next thing I knew mommy was waking me up for school. I quickly ate breakfast and put on my new clothes. Everyone at home was there to see me off to school. My daddy was even going into work late. Our entire family was at the bus stop to see me off. Even Legs was there!

All of the other neighborhood kids were also at the bus stop, and some of them had their family with them too. A few of the kids were crying along with their mothers. Daddy said, "Here comes the bus!" I could see it about a mile away, it still had three more hills to go before it made it to our stop. My stomach began to feel funny, like I was going to throw up. I knew I didn't want to do that in front of my daddy and the

33

other kids. The older kids seemed so happy to be going to school, but I wasn't happy because I loved the world I was in. By now the bus was only one hill away from us. The time I'd dreaded the most had finally came. I hugged my sister and rubbed on Legs' head. Mommy gave me a hug so tight that I could barely breathe. It felt like she gave me a hundred kisses all over my face. Daddy had to pull mommy off of me because the bus driver began to blow the horn. I looked at mommy and she was crying. So was my sister. Daddy rubbed my head and said, "I'll be right here when you get out of school."

I turned and walked onto the bus into a new world, a world that would change my life forever.

VII. Headed to School - 1971

Vincent Young

Once I was on the bus I found a seat right next to my girlfriend, Judy. She and I have been going together for about a month. Judy is a year older than me, and she's been going to a mixed school for a year. The bus is so quiet except for a few sniffles. I dare not to look back, because I might cry too. So I grab Judy's hand, and my thoughts went elsewhere. But deep down inside I feel my stomach shaking and my eyes watering. I'm so afraid right now, afraid because this is my very first time. I am alone. Then on top of that it's my first day of school. I look down at my shoes. They are still tied. I pray they stay that way, because I don't know how to tie my shoes. Mommy's words play in my mind. That I'll have to wake up my wife every morning before I go to work just to tie my shoes.

I look out the window to take my mind away. I see the Carson Farm coming up. Town isn't that far away. A while later we cross a train track. The next turn we are in town.

Once we make it into town, I see so many things, such as stores with people standing in windows. There are lots of cars, and white people are walking in and out of stores. As the bus eases through town, it seems as if every white person is staring at our bus. Only two people waved, and they were black, the only two black people I saw in town.

Once we made it to school, I'd never seen so many black and white people together in my life. As we start getting off the bus the driver said to us, "Remember your bus number." Our bus number is number eight. I didn't know this at the time. But a few years later I would be introduced to the game of pool, and it will dawn on me that the eight ball is black. Did the school know of this, or was it a coincidence that our bus was eight, and in pool, the eight ball is black? Because every person on bus #8 is black, even the driver. I still wonder about this, even to this day.

Once inside the school, everyone is moving in different directions. It looks as if someone had kicked an ant hill, with kids everywhere you looked. Judy held my hand as we walked down the hall. Most of the time she was pulling me down the hall, 'cause I was stopping and looking at the white kids. You must remember, I haven't seen a white kind my age, until I started coming to school.

Once in the room that I was assigned to, I noticed that there were no black kids. My girlfriend Judy left me alone and said she'll see me later. The teacher is white. Once everyone is seated, she explained that this is our home room. We were always to come here first. She started calling names and told them what room to go to. She finally called my name, and since I was the last one, she walked me to my class. Once there I was happy to see Linda, who stayed down the road from me. She used to be my girlfriend a long time ago. The teacher told me that her name is Ms. Ivy. She asked me my name. I took a deep breath and tried to say my name, but all that came out of my mouth was, "V... in..," because at that moment I started stuttering, real bad. Linda stood up and told the teacher that I couldn't talk. Ms. Ivy started doing sign language, but I couldn't understand her signs. So I tried to say my name again, and the same thing happened, and this time I heard someone giggling. I turned to see a white kid with his hand over his mouth and laughing. Linda got up and told the teacher my name. The teacher told me where to sit, which was right behind the kid who laughed at me. I looked around the classroom, and saw how we were sitting in rows— white, black, white, black, white, black and so on. There were five rows of six kids each, with a total of 15 white kids and 15 black kids in the classroom. We looked like the keyboard on the organ that my sister got.

Another bell rang, and Ms. Ivy told us to go outside because it's recess. Linda showed me how to get outside, but before we made it outside I saw kids standing in two different lines. One line is all black kids, but this line was for the water fountain. I found Judy outside standing in a crowd of black kids. Every kid from our area hung together at recess. Why, I don't know, but I wanted to look around to see everything here. I also noticed that the white kids stood in groups too, just like the black kids.

The only difference between a white kid and me is our skin color, hair, smell, and the way we talk. They seemed to use a lot of words with "R" in them, and the word "by" a lot.

We didn't do any school work. All we did was go to class, get our books, and meet our teachers. I noticed that all the classrooms are set up the same – black, white, black, white. I did get lucky with Linda and I having all the same classes.

Lunch finally came, and I was called to the office and given a card. The card has numbers 1 through 5 on it for each day of the week. I noticed that there are about fifty white kids and only ten black kids. The man that gave me the card said my lunch is paid for this month. I followed the other kids to the kitchen, and there I got the shock of my life! The kitchen was full of people eating. I've never seen so many people eating at the same time, but I couldn't sit where I wanted to. The teacher told you where to sit after you got your plate. They are making the black kids sit between two white kids. The food isn't good at all. I barely ate anything. No one is talking. I wanted to sit with Judy, but the teacher made me sit where she wanted me to sit. I didn't understand what was going on. Why are the teachers treating us differently from the way they are treating the white kids? The white kids raise their hands to use the bathroom, and the teacher would let them go to the bathroom by themselves. But when the black kids raise their hands to go to the bathroom the teacher would ask who else needed to use the bathroom. The teacher would take a group of us to the bathroom, and stand at the door until all of us where finished. She would only do that to the black boys and girls. Why she did this I don't know, but I do know she is treating the black kids differently from the white kids. I have so many questions for Daddy and Mommy. I still haven't said but a few words because I'm so ashamed of my stuttering. My best friend isn't with me and that's my sister. I've always had someone in my family with me until today, but today I walk alone, trying to be that little man Mommy wants me to be.

I look down, and one of my shoes is untied. How did that happen? Linda sees it too.

She came to my chair, kneeled down, and tied it for me. I don't understand this new world I'm in. I don't like it at all. I'm ready to go back to my world where everyone is the same color. The white kids seem to always be whispering, laughing, and pointing at us. I feel myself getting mad and ready to fight. I feel a hand grab my hand. I look and it's Judy, my girlfriend. All my thoughts seem to become hers. I don't know what it is. She always made my heart race and my stomach feel funny. But I still wanted to be with her forever. I can picture her tying my shoes every morning before I go to work.

The bell rang and school was finally over. The time I've waited for, which seemed like forever, was over. I go outside to find my bus. I turn to look back at the school. I see the most amazing sight I've ever seen. There looks to be about 300 kids pouring out of the school. The colors of the kids' clothing made it look as if the school was throwing up a box of coloring crayons. I found my bus #8. All I had to do was look for the black bus driver, because he is the only black man driving a school bus. I made eye contact with a few of them. The white men would spit, and the women would turn up their noses. I saw a group of white men standing around a truck, and one of them made like he was shooting a gun at us. All the other men started laughing. After about one and a half hours of riding, I finally made it home.

Everyone was there to greet me – Mommy, Daddy, my sister and Legs. I'm so happy to be back in my world! That's where I'm not treated differently, and I'm loved by everyone.

VIII. I Am Special

Vincent Young

The next few days were the same, until Thursday when I was moved to another class. This class was truly different from the other classes. The kids in this room looked like they were sick. There were more white kids, about 21 to only seven black. Some looked sleepy. Others had big heads, and three of them never stopped shaking and jerking.

The teacher talked to me as if I couldn't understand the words that were coming out of her mouth. She gave me a small book, and told me, "Anytime you have something to say you write it down in this book." All the pages were blank.

Recess finally came, and I went outside to find Judy. I found her and Linda together. I told Judy what class I was in by giving her the number. She and Linda told me that I was in a Special-Ed class. I can tell you that I didn't feel special at all.

Once I was back in the classroom, the teacher gave me some work to do. I looked at it, and it was easier than what mommy gave me. I was supposed to be in the fourth grade, but if this is fourth grade work I figured I'd be okay, because I could already add, subtract, and read the "Dick and Jane and Spot" books.

I hit a white kid today for calling me a nigger. Why he called me that I don't know, but all I could think about was what daddy told me, "Never let anyone call you a nigger," so I popped him a good one, because he'd just walked up to me in the kitchen and said, "Nigger, what's your name?" I noticed how quiet it got in the kitchen, and everyone was looking at us. The white kid hollered so loudly that you would've thought that a turtle had his big toe. Someone grabbed me from behind, and I looked around to see it was our bus driver. He also worked in the kitchen as a dishwasher.

I was taken to the office, and the teacher told this man that I'd started the fight. I tried to tell them what happened, but I started stuttering. They didn't bring the other kid to the office. Why, I don't know.

I was taken to my classroom after I ate lunch, back to the same old class, "Special-Ed" in room 19. I stayed there all day, not really doing anything, and I hated this room after my first day. I didn't know anyone in this class, and the only time I got to see my girlfriend and friends was at recess.

School was finally over, and the ride on old bus #8 was long and quiet. Once off the bus, the only one waiting for me was Legs. All the other kids spoke to Legs as they walked by.

A lot of things were going through my mind, all of them about what happened at school, especially about the class I was in. Once I was inside the house, I got my sister to translate my thoughts for me. She told our mother what I was talking about, and mommy then said, "I'll take you to school tomorrow. I didn't think mommy would ride the school bus with me, but the next morning she did. Mommy and my sister both got on the bus with me. I was sort of happy, because my sister was going to school with me, but I wondered how they both would get home, because daddy was at work. I heard mommy tell daddy, "You're not going to miss work!"

I still sat on the seat with Judy, and we held hands. Mommy knew that Judy was my girlfriend. Everyone on the bus respected my mother, saying, "Yes, ma'am," or calling her Mrs. Young. This was because every mother in our area had permission to whip each other's kids, so no matter whose house you were at, you had to be on your best behavior.

Once we made it to school, mommy, my sister, and I went to the office. The lady behind the desk asked my mommy if she was there to register us for school. "No," said mommy, "I'm here to find out who put my son in the Special-Ed class!" A man came out and showed us into his office, where he explained to my mother why I was in that class. It was because I couldn't talk. My mommy told him that I could talk. I just had a stuttering problem. She also told him that I could do seventh grade work because she'd home-schooled me from the age of two. Mommy demanded that I be taken out of that class. The man said he would, and then asked her about my sister. Mommy told him that my sister was only eight, and would start school next year. That sparked another argument, which led to mommy telling him that no one will tell her how to raise her kids.

Mommy led us both to the door by our hands. While we were leaving, the man asked about me going to class, and she told him that I wasn't going to school that day.

Mommy took us to her friend's house, which wasn't far from the school. Once there, my sister and I stayed outside and watched the cars go by. We also saw a lot of squirrels, and I wished I had my .22 pump. I didn't, so I played at shooting them while my sister kept count and made sure I didn't shoot the same squirrels twice. I was up to seven in no time.

Mommy came outside and sat on the porch with her friend, Mary. Mommy said daddy was coming to pick us up. I hoped in his airplane. I sat and wondered how he was coming to get us. I looked around, but the only place to land was in the street. Plus we had mommy with us, and I'd never heard her talk about flying in a plane with daddy, so I knew right then that we'd be riding in the car.

Daddy picked us up, and on the drive home, Mommy told him what had happened that day. We made a stop and daddy bought ice cream for all of us. Mommy even told him about the fight I had. All he did was look in the rear view mirror and smiled, giving me a wink.

Finally at home, I changed out of my school clothes, and then headed to the barn to play with my pet pig, Legs.

IX. Changes

Vincent Young

Months later, things are changing fast, with everything and everyone. I feel my heart filling with anger every day, because I don't like the way I'm being treated and looked at constantly. On Tuesday morning, it's me and Legs again, waiting at the end of the road for the bus. When the bus pulled up, I saw that someone had painted this on the side: *NIGGERS ONLY.* Some of the windows are knocked out, too. The last six seats in the rear are empty, three on each side, and the back windows are gone. For the first time, I can't sit with my girlfriend, Judy. I looked out from the bus as we pulled away, and I saw Legs heading back to the house.

People are staring at our bus as we go through town, and the same thing happened when we got to school, but these people were pointing their fingers and laughing at us.

Daddy had told me, "Son, people will hate you because of the color of your skin. Not only white people, but some black people will hate you too."

I ignored them, got off the bus, and went to my class, which was no longer in the Special Ed room. Now I'm in the class with Judy. We were holding hands and walking to class when she said, "Why did they do that to our bus?" I shrugged my shoulders to indicate, "I don't know."

I only spoke about 1100 words in school from the fourth to the ninth grade, because I didn't want to be laughed at. When I was with Judy, or anyone else I knew, they always did all the talking. I just listened. Judy knew some, but not all, of the sign language I used with my sister. That's probably why I felt so angry inside, because I couldn't express myself in words. Remember that I'm a black kid born in 1962, and I'm going to an integrated Mississippi school in 1971. It seemed that every white person hated every black person. That helped me stay angry.

A fight broke out on the playground, with this much bigger white kid jumping on a much smaller black kid. I didn't know the black kid, because he wasn't from where I lived.

The next thing I knew, the teacher was pulling me off the white kid. They took me to the office where the principal started fussing at me. But then a black man walked in and said, "Let me talk to him." He came over to me. "My name is Kennedy. I'm the superintendent of this school. Tell me what happened." I felt I could trust this man, so I told him what I'd seen. "The teachers ignored the fight until I jumped on the white kid."

Mr. Kennedy listened, and then said, "Tell your daddy that I said hello. You're going to be just like him." What surprised me about him was that he was so nice to me. And he

41

didn't laugh at me when I began to stutter badly. Even so, I told him what happened.

Judy was mad at me when I got back to class. She was angry because I was fighting. I looked down, and my shoe was untied. She saw it too. "Put your foot in my lap," she said, and she tied it for me, which always made me feel good, because it's her way to show how she cared about me. I liked that. A lot.

By age eleven, I was known by my friends as "The Fighter." That became my nickname, because from my first day in school, my life took a path where I didn't want it to go.

My mommy and daddy heard me plead for them to take me out of school. They waited too late. The damage was already done. One word, one wrong word in school would make me fight. That word was "nigger". I can still hear my daddy say, "Never let anyone get away with calling you a nigger."

I'm doing well in school, and my grades are good. Every report card earns me five dollars from my mommy. The main problem that I had was in English where I had to read out loud. My teacher made me read out a whole paragraph, and that would take me between ten and fifteen minutes. But out teacher, Ms. Lancaster, always made me read each and every word. I'd stutter and hear snickers. When I'd finish, I'd look at Judy and see her crying. I'd told her, after my first time reading, that it hurt me so badly that I was crying on the inside. And I was very angry.

I felt that I could only count on Judy and my family. And Legs. My pet pig would be there waiting for me every single school day, morning and afternoon. I knew she'd be there at the end of the road. Mommy told me, "I can tell the time by watching Legs."

School had become for me the most hated place to be. I told my sister all about how bad it was, because next year she'd be riding with me to school.

I won a lot of fights from the fourth grade up to my ninth grade, mostly because those kids fought differently from us country kids. All they wanted to do was play "Dare Fights", which goes like this. They'd draw a line in the dirt and dare the other kid to cross it. Or, they'd put a stick on their shoulder and dare the other to knock it off.

I took advantage of that kind of dare-fighting by drawing the line and daring the kid to cross it. My trick was to stand a foot behind the line. I'd give him one "Dare you!" with just enough room for him to step across, and I'd make sure that the line was no longer than a foot. When he raised his step over I'd pop him a good one. Every time they'd fall down from the lick, because it's hard to stand on only one leg after taking an upper-cut punch.

The "stick-on-the-shoulder" thing was even easier. The kid placed the stick on his shoulder and dared me to knock it off. I'd punch him, the stick would fall, and it's over with. I won many more fights than I lost, but all this fighting changed me into a person that I didn't want to be. I was so full of anger that something inside me had changed.

42

My sister's first day did not go well. She told me at recess, "Some white kid pulled my hair." She pointed him out to me. I walked up to him, and without a word, I hit him hard and knocked him down. "You leave my sister alone!" Everyone else stood around looking. They took me and my sister to the office, where she told the principal what had happened to her, and what she'd told me about it. The principal told me that he was going to call my mother and tell her what I'd done.

About the sixth grade, I was weary of my anger and tired of hurting others, and unhappy that my fourth period class was in a downtown Psych doctor's office. I could not talk cause of my stuttering, so I just sat there for fifty minutes and listened to this woman tell me what was wrong with me, which she didn't know. They always called my mother every time I got in trouble. They'd call my sister to translate my sign language, and they'd call my mommy with the hope that she'd whip me. What they failed to realize was that my mommy and daddy didn't care about my fighting, as long as it was white kids and not black kids. With that encouragement, I upped my fighting skills, knocking them down like bowling pins.

I got expelled, for three days. I was happy with that, because instead of school, I was out hunting with Legs in tow. It's hard to hunt with a pig. Legs wasn't fast enough to run down a rabbit. But she understood my hand signals well. Stop, go, and lay down. She was smart. Smarter than those white kids, I thought. She could always find a rabbit hole, and I'd become a pretty good shot with my .22 pump. Way better than school!

Me and Legs spent a lot of time together for those three days. We even went swimming in a pond not far from the house. That was the day mommy took us fishing with her. My sister, Legs, and me could not get in the water until mommy was through fishing. My sister would get on Leg's back, and Legs would swim all the way across the pond with my sister on her back. We truly had a fun day. Even mommy got in the water. She raced me and Legs across the pond. I think she let us win just to see the smile on my face. Mommy was soaking wet from head to toe. She seemed not to care about it, or her dress being wet. My sister and mommy was in front of me and Legs. She and mommy skipped together all the way home. Mommy caught six fish that day, and that's what we had for lunch. Even Legs got a fish sandwich with ketchup on it.

X. True Pain

Vincent Young

I can only remember crying twice between ages six and eleven. Yes, I got whippings, but I always held back my tears. I only cried on the inside. I could not, and would not, let my mother see me cry. The reason is that I'm her "Little Man", and a man does not cry.

I learned from my father to never let anyone see you cry, because crying is a sign of softness and weakness, and a man is neither. But it was something about death that tore me up. I cried like a baby when Truck died. Now I'm crying again.

It's 1973, a slightly rainy day in October. It was cold, too. I didn't want to go to school, but I had to. Me, my sister and Legs stood waiting for the bus. When it came I tried to get on, but Legs blocked my way. I pointed towards the house, and Legs moved out of the way. Once I was on the bus, I looked out the back window to see if Legs was heading to the house, but not this morning. Legs was following us down the road. I told my sister, and she asked the bus driver to stop so I could make Legs go back home. He did so, and said, "Boy, you got one minute." I stepped off the bus, and beckoned for Legs to come to me. When she did, I rubbed her ears and pointed towards the house again. This time, Legs went back towards the house. That made me think, that before I got on the bus this morning, I didn't rub Leg's ears, which I did every morning before getting on the bus, and every evening when I got off the bus. To this day I wonder how far Legs would've followed us just to have her ears rubbed.

I'm in third period when I'm called to the office. I go in and find my sister and mommy there crying. The first thought that came to my mind was that Legs was dead. Mommy saw me and pulled me into her arms, where she told me the worst news I'd ever hear in my young life, "Your daddy was killed this morning in a car wreck." I didn't cry right then because I didn't want to believe what she was telling me. My daddy is the toughest man I know. He's the best daddy in the world. He cannot be dead. How can I become what he is if he's dead?

We leave the school and head home. Mommy's sister is driving. Mommy has stopped crying some, but my sister is still crying.

Our yard at home is full of cars and people. It's no longer raining, but it's still cool a bit. I got out of the car and headed straight for the barn to find Legs. I could hear Mommy calling me, but I couldn't turn around. I couldn't stop the tears running down my face. In the barn I found Legs, and I sat down beside her where I cried like a baby. Legs laid her head in my lap, and I rubbed her ears as I cried. I heard someone coming and calling my name. It was my Uncle "Big John", and he is very big. Uncle John is a logger. I've seen him pick up a tree and put it on his shoulder, tote it to his truck and throw it onto it. Uncle John spoke to me and Legs, sitting down next to us. He told me

45

not to worry, that God had called daddy to heaven, because God needed some help to fight the devil. Somehow that made sense to me, because I knew my daddy could fight.

Me and Legs left the barn with Uncle John, and we headed to the house where we all went inside, including Legs. Mommy didn't say anything about Legs being in the house, so I took her to my sister's room where she and my cousins were at. My Aunt Molly hollered, "Vincent! Get that pig out of the house!" Mommy said, "Mary, this is my house, and no one can tell me what can or can't be here. Leave Legs alone." So I kept going with Legs straight to my sister's room. Aunt Mary apologized to my mommy, and they embraced each other. Uncle John started doing what he did best and that's telling stories. I don't know if the stories he told were true, but they always had everybody laughing.

Like the one he told about him, my daddy, and some friend, and how they were out riding around one night. The police pulled them over for wobbling a little bit. Everyone in the car was drunk, even my daddy who just happened to be driving. Uncle John told everyone to be quiet and let him do the talking. My daddy started babbling when the officer came up to the driver's window. Daddy sounded like a deaf and dumb person. "What's wrong with him?" asked the officer, and Uncle John said, "He's deaf and dumb. We're being nice to him and teaching him how to drive." The police officer said, "Well, now. That's right nice of you boys, but ya'll hurry up and get this deaf and dumb son-of-a-bitch home before he runs over somebody!" Uncle John said they were all so drunk that they slept in the car. He told us that if the police had told them to get out of the car there was no way they could've done it. That's how drunk they were.

I noticed how quiet Legs had become once we got into the house. I couldn't keep her in my sister's room. All Legs wanted to do was lay in Mommy's room extra quiet like, not even grunting like most pigs do. I wondered, "Did Legs know that God had called Daddy to help Him fight the devil?" I tried to get Legs out of Mommy's room, but she wouldn't budge at all. Then Mommy came in and Legs got up and went straight to her. Mommy started rubbing Legs' ears and said, "Come on, baby. Let me get you something to eat." Nobody said a word as they watched a fully grown pig follow Mommy into the kitchen. We didn't go to school the next day or even the next seven days after.

XI. Funeral

Vincent Young

I sat fidgeting in my clothes on the day of my daddy's funeral. Everything seemed so tight, even my socks. I wanted badly to take off my suit. I saw Uncle John drive up in his truck with his wife, Aunt Mary. Everyone came out of the house when we were ready to leave, even Legs. I thought she would be headed to the barn, but I was wrong. Mommy said, "Don't be rubbing her ears, because she's going with us." Mommy told me to put Legs on the truck, which I was happy to do. I got the walk-board out of the back of the truck and walked Legs up into the truck. Instead of riding in the car to the funeral home, I rode in the back of the truck with Legs.

Once we got to the funeral home, we all loaded into the car for the longest, slowest, and most painful ride of my life. I could feel the water building up behind my eyes like it was looking for a small crack to be released down my face.

When we arrived at the church, there were people everywhere, and they all looked so sad. What truly shocked me was that there were white people there. I didn't know that my daddy had so many white friends. So why did it seem to me that he'd hated white people? But here they were, standing out in front of the church, greeting Mommy and nodding to her. It looked to be about 500 people there, about 150 of them were white. Legs had to stay outside under the shade tree. As the service started so did the water pressure behind my eyes. I couldn't hold it back as the service continued, and I broke down in front of all these people, which I didn't care about because I was only twelve years old. My crying started my mommy and sister crying too.

All I could think about was why did God need my daddy? He could have got Mr. Richard or any other daddy.

There was a lot of noise at the back of the church, and I knew what it was as I turned to look back. There was Legs running down the aisle in the middle of the church. The preacher didn't say a words as he watched Legs come to my mommy's side. Mommy rubbed her head and said, "Lay down." To my surprise, Legs did what Mommy said, and here I'd thought that Legs only did what me and my sister told her to do. She didn't make a sound throughout the rest of the service. I noticed that her eyes were moist like she was crying too. As we got up to follow the casket out of the church, Mommy led the way, followed by my sister, Legs, and then myself.

The hurting part was watching them lower my daddy's casket into the ground. I knew then I'd never see my daddy again because I remember when Truck was being lowered into the ground.

The last thing I could remember my daddy telling me the day he got killed was, "Always take care of your sister and mommy."

After the funeral was over, we piled back into the car and headed home, where the yard was full of people and the kitchen was full of food. You just name it and you probably would've found it in the kitchen that day.

Mommy came out and sat on the porch and talked to just about everyone. She brought out a few slices of pie and cake for Legs, because Legs was right by my mommy's side.

I wonder, "Does Legs understand what's happened? Does she know that Daddy is dead?" I would motion for Legs to come to me, and she would, but she wouldn't come off the porch because she wanted to stay around Mommy. I wondered to myself that night what it would be like now. Would I wake up and listen for Daddy to be walking around the house? I cried off and on all night, especially after Mommy told us everything, like why so many white people came to daddy's funeral. Daddy had many friends, black and white, and through this fighting career he met and talked to thousands of people. She also told me that she always worried about my daddy when he flew airplanes, but she never thought that he would die in a car wreck.

I'll never understand the wreck. They say that Daddy was sitting at a red light, when out of nowhere a car came up from behind and hit Daddy's car, pushing him out into traffic where he was hit on the driver's side by another car, which killed him.

The next morning the house was so quiet. I laid there and listened to it. All I could hear was Legs grunting every now and then. I got up and got dressed. Now I must do what daddy did every morning, which was feed the chickens and pigs. I went to the living room and my mommy sat there crying. I put my arm around her and cried too. She asked me, "What are you doing up?" I told her, "Me and Legs are going to feed the pigs and chickens." She smiled and said, "You and Legs hurry up. I'm fixing to cook breakfast."

XII. Runaway

Vincent Young

For the next few days I did my job every morning, me and Legs fed the pigs and chickens. Feeding the other hogs was a task because they will run over you trying to get to the trough, but Legs seemed to always stand between me and them, and when they got too close she would grunt real loud. They would stop and back away from the trough.

Then we would go in the house and eat breakfast. Yes, Legs would eat what I ate— rice, biscuit, eggs and bacon. Then I'd take a bath and get ready for school.

Around 10:00 in the morning, at school, I would get so sleepy. That was because I was getting up every morning at 5 A.M. That way I'd have time to feed the chickens, gather the eggs, and feed the hogs. I am becoming the "little man" that I've always wanted to be for my mommy. But I didn't want it like this. I wanted my daddy with me. Why did God have to take my daddy away from me?

The idea hit me how I could be right beside my daddy, fighting along with him and God, fighting the devil! There was only one way for me to do that, and I did.

At least three times a week, I got into a fight I had to show God that I'm a good fighter and pray He'll come get me.

After a few months of this all, I got was in trouble. I got a whipping for fighting Larry, Charles, and Bobby, because they are black like me. God didn't call on me in those few months, and that only made me more angry.

My job of feeding the animals was taken over by Uncle John, but Legs and me still got up at the same time of 5 A.M., to go and get the eggs out of the hen house, which was very easy.

I don't know what was happening to me, but I knew something was wrong inside. The doctor I was seeing during my fourth period class told me that I was doing all my fighting because I missed my daddy. Maybe she was right, but she did not know why. The path I'd taken that day my daddy died will lead me to a place I wish on no one. My violent ways were pushing me to the point of no return.

That was the day mommy told me and my sister that we were moving to town, and that she would sell all the hogs and chickens. I looked at Legs and knew then that we must run away.

That night I packed two pairs of pants and underwear. I grabbed two loaves of bread, one for me and one for Legs. I stopped by the hen house and got a few eggs, and headed to the barn to get Legs.

49

Me and Legs hit the woods and headed for the pond. I knew my way to my grand mommy's house, but we had to stay out of sight in the woods. I'd also brought two quilts, one for me and one for Legs.

I didn't remember the night ever being this dark, but it was darker than dark, and the noise in the woods was a little louder. I could hear something moving around me and Legs, like something was following us. We would stop walking and it would stop walking. We'd move a little faster and it would move faster, too. Once we made it to the open space by the pond I no longer heard it behind us.

Me and Legs put up a little camp by the pond. I ate two pieces of bread, and Legs ate two pieces, too.

I didn't sleep at all that night. I covered Legs up with one quilt and I took the other. Early the next morning, we struck out again, and headed for my grand mommy's house. We had only fifteen miles to go before we got there. Me and Legs covered good ground on the second day, but it still seemed that we were miles away from her house. That night, every star in the sky was lit up. Me and Legs made camp, and I was asleep as soon as I laid down.

Legs woke me up while it was still dark, but the sun would be up soon. It was day three and it would be our last night in the woods. I rode on Leg's back most of the day, and all of the way, until we got to the rock-road. This was the road that will lead me to where I want to be.

We got to grand mommy's house, and I could see daddy's truck in the yard. My sister was outside, and Legs started running to her. I knew then, that Mommy was inside waiting on me. I heard my granddaddy yell, "Boy, get your ass in the house! You done had you mommy worried for three days about you, boy!" My sister started playing with Legs, while I headed into the house. When I walked in I got the biggest hug and kisses from mommy, who told me that she wasn't going to whip me as long as I promised not to ever run away again. Mommy said, "Baby, you could've been eaten by a panther or killed by stray dogs and wild hogs!" "Why do we have to move?" I asked her. "It hurts me too much to live in that house without daddy," she said. "Can we take Legs with us to town?" I asked. "Legs is staying here with grand mommy and we can come visit her every weekend," she answered.

Mommy made me take a bath, fed me real good, and I slept like a baby. I had laid in the woods that first night looking at the dark, starless sky and wondered why all the angels were asleep. Why wasn't one of them watching over me? Daddy had told me that the stars are angels watching over every kid in the world.

Granny woke me the next morning to eat breakfast, and she always made me flapjacks. I asked could I get some for Legs and she said yes, so after I finished eating I took Legs five flapjacks.

XIII. The Move - 1974

Vincent Young

The day of the move was not what I expected. There was everyone helping us move. We had a train of trucks behind us following us to our new home. The most hurtful thing about the move was that I could not take Legs with us. We had to leave her at my grand mommy's house. Once we were at our new home, I noticed people walking up and down the street. Another thing I hated was how close the houses were together. I could look out our window and see into the next house. Even if the people are black, it was the way they looked at us.

Our new house wasn't as big as the one we'd left. This one had one bathroom and our old house had two. Now all three of us would have to use the same bathroom. When we finished unpacking, I went outside and sat on the porch. I felt I was in a world that I wanted no part of, but mommy had forced me into this world. Why did she sell our house and all our animals? I'm not old enough to say or ask why. Me and my sister are alone a lot at night. Mommy and her friend go somewhere at night, and some girl came over to stay with us until she came home.

The babysitter's name is Penny, and she's only three years older than me. I must say, she is the most beautiful girl I've ever seen.

After about a month in our new home, I had made a few friends and also had a few fights. They gave me the nickname, "Country Boy". I only talked with my sister, and hardly said anything to my friends. I was boiling inside and ready to blow. I was upset about moving, about the death of my daddy, and about leaving Legs behind. I'm a twelve year old boy missing his daddy very much.

We're still going to the same school, only this time we walked there. So, every morning I would wait on bus #8 to pull up, and when it did, I'd wait for Judy to get off. I explained to her as best as I could that I didn't like it at all, and that I'd wanted to stay in our house and not his new one.

A few weeks later, I noticed Judy was drifting away from me. She no longer held my hand or rubbed my neck. I came to find out that she and Larry were talking, and that only added to my anger. Everything seemed to be turning against me and causing me more pain.

Mommy asked me, "What's wrong?" I guess she could see my pain. I told her only half the truth, because maybe she wouldn't understand. I told her about how Judy was treating me and how I missed Legs. She told me I have many years ahead of me and I'll find another girlfriend. "Go get your sister and meet me at the car," she said, and when I did, she came out and told us, "We're going to grand mommy's house." I could hardly wait to get there, 'cause I haven't seen Legs in two weeks. When we pulled up in

51

the yard, Legs came running from behind the house to greet us. We played with Legs before going in the house, me, my sister and mommy. We must've been playing a long time because grand mommy came outside and said, "Ya'll would rather come see that hog than come give your grand mommy a hug!" Me and my sister gave grand mommy and granddaddy a hug. Then I ran straight back to Legs with my sister in tow.

The most hurtful part about visiting grand mommy was when the time came to leave, 'cause leaving Legs behind would hurt me so much. As we pulled out of the driveway, Legs would look like her world was coming to an end. Legs always trotted behind the car all the way to the end of the road. That was the last time we saw Legs alive. She died a week later. From loneliness, I believe, and because she had no one to play with and rub her ears. Legs missed seeing how much she was loved. Legs didn't get the great funeral like Truck, because daddy was the one who did Truck's funeral. But I can say that granddaddy did do a good job. He even got a real preacher to say a few words over Leg's coffin. I just assumed that the reason Legs died is that we weren't there for her.

I didn't cry out at Leg's funeral. Instead, I cried within. After the death of my daddy I promised myself that I wouldn't cry out again. Little did I know by doing this, It would cost me my happiness, my freedom, and my love.

ERNEST HERRING
#41881

Earnest Herring was raised in a poverty-stricken home with four sisters and five brothers in Edwards, Mississippi near Vicksburg. He dropped out of school in the eighth grade, and is currently serving forty mandatory years for sexual assault.

Drifting into Darkness

Ernest Herring

She would hum a spiritual hymn, and the foreboding evil spirit would leave.

It was the year 1962; I was born black and poverty-stricken in the city of Vicksburg, Mississippi. The most memorable account of my life begins around 1974. I was twelve years old and had five (5) brothers and four (4) sisters. We lived in a country town named Edwards. Edwards is 18 miles east of Vicksburg, near the Big Black River. The Big Black River connects to the Mississippi River, which is commonly known as Big Muddy.

We were a large family, but not dysfunctional. My father's name is, Willie, born in mid-1920s, he had only a fourth grade education. I don't know why he didn't complete school, and I didn't ask, I was a little bit fearful of him. Not that he abused me or anything like that; it was a reverential fear. He earned our respect because he stood about 6ft 8in, weighing 210lbs, with big strong hands.

Moreover, we revered him for being a man of determination: good hustler, protector, and great provider. He worked at a saw-mill named Anderson Tully Lumber Company in Vicksburg, Mississippi, located on the banks of the Big Muddy. His job as a saw-man didn't pay more than minimum wage. Thus, to supplement his income he would exercise his hustling skills, like going out to the Old Barn and firing up the whiskey still.

Sometimes he would even allow me to tag along, just to keep him company. He would also buy a truck load of dry wood, wood too short for lumber, but can be used for firewood. He would buy an oversized load for three dollars employee's discount, bring the top half home, and sell a regular pickup truck load to several neighbors, regular customers.

Furthermore, when Mama would complain about the money being short, in late fall he would go out to the shed and get his Homelite C-72 chainsaw, gather my three older brothers and me into the Chevy pickup, and we'd go to work in the forest to cut and haul firewood all day. I've always had a fascination about anything mechanical. One day my father cut the chainsaw off to do some wood splitting. I decided that when he gets ready to start the chainsaw, I was going to assist him by starting it up for him. He let me...But to my surprise, when I pulled the string, the compression was so strong it snatched the string out of my hand! From that time onward, I didn't mess with daddy's chainsaw.

Sometime during wood cutting season, it would rain four or five days straight. The ground would get too soft for the pickup to go down in the low area without getting stuck. So daddy would send one of us to the stable to fetch the mule, the mule's name was Jeannie. She was young, intelligent and hyper; and she'd never been ridden by anyone. So I would put the gear on her and walk her out to the forest to meet Daddy.

After Daddy had thrown a tree, he would holler and wave his hand, signaling me to bring Jeannie. I would back Jeannie up to a log about 25ft. long. Daddy would tie a chain around the log. Then he would tell Jeannie, "Get up, girl!" She'd jump and snatch the log! And I would take off running leading her through the woods to high ground. My other brothers Willie Jr., Charles, and Donald would be on high ground cutting the log down to about two feet long, firewood size. Once the pickup was loaded, Willie Jr. would haul the wood to Daddy's customers.

The Primitive Life

Our living conditions were somewhat primitive. The house was shot-gun style with no running water, nor indoor restroom. When my sisters had to use the facility, they had a night jar in their room. When my brothers or I had to go to the toilet, we went out back to the outhouse.

When it was time to bathe, my brothers or I would go outside and get water from the faucet outdoors in the yard, build a fire around a big black 15 or 20 gallon cooking pot, and heat the water in the yard. Once the water gets hot, I would dip a five gallon bucket into the pot and carry my bath water indoors. Then I would pour a mixture of hot and cold water in a number three tub and take my bath. When it was cold and rainy outdoors, I would bring the water in and heat it in a tea kettle on an iron wood heater or the fireplace.

My sisters would do the same before bedtime. And also again when morning came. Mama was more strict on the girl's bathing than us boys. My mother is a God-fearing woman. What I mean by God-fearing is, her Christian roots run deep, and she has a high regard and respect for God's word— The Bible. Although Daddy believed in God, Mama was a Giant Prayer Warrior!

Mother's name is Ella Mae. She is a homemaker, commonly known as a housewife. She's an early bird— early to bed, early to rise. She would rise around 4:00 A.M. and start breakfast and fix Daddy's lunch. We had a woodstove...Therefore she had to go outside and get kindling to jumpstart the fire. She usually had breakfast ready around 5:00 A.M. every weekday. The family usually ate around the table. Then daddy heads off to work at 6:15 A.M. every morning. After breakfast, Mama would prepare us for school, and afterwards, watch us as we stood at the fork of the road waiting on the bus. She would begin cleaning the house and laundry, while at the same time humming spiritual hymns. One day, I had a bad cold and was home from school. I said to her, "Why you not sing instead of humming, because your voice sounds wonderful?" She said, "She hums when her spirit is troubled, and Satan's angels cannot understand what she's saying or thinking."

56

Killing Season

It is late fall, the family is preparing for the holidays. Daddy would take my brothers and me turkey and geese hunting. Since we didn't have but one gun, he would let each of us take turns bringing down geese or turkeys. After returning home, we would clean our kill and put it in the freezer until Thanksgiving Eve.

The weekend before Thanksgiving, Daddy would go out to the hog pin and cut a hog's throat, afterwards that hog would get up and run around the pin with blood running from its throat until it fell dead. Daddy would build a big fire around a 25 or 30 gallon black cooking pot and boil water there in the back yard. While waiting for the water to come to a boil, he would place the dead hog into a 55 gallon barrel with a 45 degree angle and pour hot water in and take his butcher knife and scrape all the hair off. Next he would take the hog and cut into the muscle/tendon behind each lower back leg, then take a hickory stick about two feet long with a sharp point on each end, and push through the muscle/tendon. He then placed a rope around the hickory stick and through the chain horse, then hoist the hog upside down. Once the hog is hanging, he then takes the butcher knife, and cuts it open from the throat to the tail— exposing all internal organs.

Mama and my four sisters: Princess, Sharon, Dorothy, and Bertha gathered around a table there in the back yard, with sharp butcher knives. They would cut the outside layer of the carcass into small square or cube shapes, behind that they would dip the water out of the black pot Daddy used, and put the square shape meat in and cook until it turned into lard. When all the lard is cooked from the meat, what is left is called pork skins. Nothing is thrown away. The intestines are separate, cleansed and washed thoroughly before cooking and eating.

The Holiday Season

Mama and my sisters would take the turkey, geese, and hen out of the freezer. Then Mama would start with laying the turkey flat on its back, legs in the air. She would cut the turkey in half, debone it, and place a special kind of homemade stuffing all over it. Additionally, she'd take a geese and lay it flat on its back on top of the turkey, cut it in half, debone it, and place stuffing all over it. Finally, she took the hen, placed it on its back on top of the geese, cut it in half, deboned it, and placed stuffing all over it. Furthermore, she'd take the turkey and close it, enclosing both geese and hen. My sister would then place a cooking pot on top of the turkey, while Mama flipped the birds and pot off its back to its front. They would pour chicken stock, and all kind of spices in the pot, and place the birds in the oven for 6 ½ hours, and the birds were cooked through.

After the turkey has cooked long enough (which was a very long time!) it is removed. Therefore, Mama and my sisters could proceed to cooking cakes and pies, and sharing recipes. On Thanksgiving Day we came together in praise, prayer and feast. Mama would start by singing a hymn or two, and my sisters would join her. Daddy would give the Thanksgiving prayer and benediction. Then we would feast serving ourselves as we pass the food dish around the dinner table.

Christmas is also a time we came together in praise, prayer, and feast. However, Mama added plenty of fruits, nuts, candy and homemade ice cream. Moreover, Daddy and Mama would take us shopping in the city of Vicksburg. Daddy took me over to Western Auto Hardware Store, and bought me a new, red, 3-speed, Western Flyer bicycle. That bike was the most memorable thing I've ever owned at twelve years old.

Broken Heart

It was now early spring, the beginning of the end of the school year. The school's faculty organized a field trip just before summer break. We all boarded three Continental Trailway buses, and went to an amusement park across Lake Pontchartrain Bridge close to New Orleans, Louisiana.

Upon arriving at the park resort, we exited the buses. The teachers implemented a plan to keep everyone together; we were placed in groups and pairs. My partner's name was Rosia Ducker... she is the daughter of a faculty member. Her personality was attractive, reserved and modest.

I was excited, yet afraid of her. Because I've never been that close to a girl. She and I did everything together from the carousel to the gyro wheel. We were inseparable and I was filled with glee.

Although Rosia was unaware, and I tried to maintain my composure...I was beginning to have a crush on her, and the feelings I was having for her were something I couldn't explain. The irony is, I wanted my feelings to stop; but, on the other hand, I want them to continue in spite of the risk of me being rejected by her.

Well, the field trip finally ended and everyone returned to their classes doing their usual thing. However, I wasn't the same. The time Rosia and I shared together actually had an emotional affect on me I just couldn't shake. In fact, my thoughts of her persisted daily. So I begin to reason with myself, and decided to tell her my feelings.

It was around lunch time, the other students and I were walking to the cafeteria, and I noticed students stopping to read a poster sign on the bulletin board. It read, "There will be a student dance contest in the school's gymnasium Friday 8:00 P.M.— 10:00 P.M.; All Contestants must Apply at the Principal's office." I could dance, but not good enough to compete. Thus, I didn't apply. Of course, I thought this would be a great opportunity to express my feelings to Rosia. There were still a few days before the dance. So I was on the lookout for Rosia to ask her, was she going?

It was evening and school was ended for the day. I was headed home riding my bicycle, as I was leaving the school yard I saw Rosia walking towards the school bus, and immediately...My heart skipped a beat, and started racing! Then I thought, I need to holler at her to ask, is she going to the dance? Suddenly...I was struck with timidity, again! It seems every time I'd get close to her, my emotions would go crazy— yet and still, I had to battle with them, encouraging myself saying, "It's now or never"!

I took off on my bike across the school yard. As I approached her, I hollered her name exuberantly— attracting attention. She looked towards me enthusiastically anticipating any words I had to say. I said to her..."Did you not hear about the school's dance contest?" She said, "Yes." I say, "...Are you going?" She said, "Yes...Are you?" I said, "Yes...But, only because you'll be there." She gazed at me with a smirk on her face— seemingly excited by my comment. I wanted to say more but her bus was about to leave. She boarded the bus and I continued my journey home. It seemed from the expression on her face, and the few words she uttered, that I'd won her heart.

Friday night just couldn't come fast enough, and it was now only Thursday. I looked for her all day at school, but to no avail. I couldn't call her by phone— my parents couldn't afford that luxury...Besides, I didn't know her number anyway. I considered riding over to her house on my bicycle, but the journey was too far for me to make it back home before dark. Mama and Daddy were very strict about me coming home on my bike after dark. To ease my anxiety, I went down to the ball court and played a few games of ball on the dirt court. After that, that was able to relax and get some sleep.

When Friday night finally arrived...I pressed my pants with the iron, while the water outside in the pot was getting hot for my bath. My hair was nappy, so I ran my mother's hot comb over it, until I had an afro style. I hitched a ride to the dance with my older brother, Willie Jr. His old car was beat-up and not very solid, but we made it there just the same.

When I arrived at the dance, I saw Rosia sitting with her mother at the front doors. Her mother was a faculty member who was in charge of collecting money for the school's programs. The moment Rosia saw me, her eyes lit-up like a lightning bug! I didn't want her mother to notice our attraction to each other. So I just smiled at her and eased on back to the bleachers section. After about 45 minutes or so, I decided to find my way to the concession stand hoping to see Rosia, and I did see her. When she saw me, she came over where I was standing. I offered to buy her a soda, she accepted. I begin to compliment her attire...She seemed pleased I paid such close attention.

As our night continued, I begin telling her of the strong feelings of intense interest and affection I felt towards her, and I wanted us to always be friends...She agreed, and said her feelings were mutual. But the expression on her face seemed sad. I looked into her eyes and said to her, "What's wrong...Is it something I said?" She said her mother got a better job in a higher position, and they were in the process of moving to another state. My heart was broken, which was my fear from the beginning. I gave her my address, and we said our goodbyes.

Planting Season

We had over 40 acres of land, but Daddy only farmed about ten. He'd say, "Ten acres is all we need and all he have time to care for." So he would send my brothers and me out to the pastureland to fetch Jennie, where she would be grazing. Daddy had already paid a tractor owner to come by and till the section of land. So we hitched Jennie up to the harrow and took turns dragging debris to the end of the field where Daddy was burning it. We'd work there in the field all day.

The following weekend we would fetch Jennie again, hitch her to a plow and row up the field. Finally...if the weather was good enough, Daddy, Mama, all my sisters, my brothers and me would go out to the field, and start planting - we each had our own row. We worked the field all day.

Back to School and Revival

Daddy and Mama would take us all to the city of Vicksburg to buy our back-to-school clothes. We would spend half a day walking from store to store in search of the best deals and sales.

When headed home after shopping, Daddy would stop by a restaurant and give us five dollars each. We would purchase our order and eat ourselves full riding in the front and back of the pickup truck traveling on the interstate.

Not long after I turned twelve, Mama told Daddy it was time for me and two of my other brothers to join the church. We climbed into the pickup truck and went to church every night for a whole week— they called it Revival. At the end of the week, the pastor gave an extra-long service...He extended an invitation to come to Jesus, if we desired. Both my brothers and I accepted the invitation, and we seated up front on the mourner's bench— it was a Friday night. That Sunday, we all gathered outside the church and walked across a pastureland to a pond and there we were baptized.

Although I was sincere when I accepted the pastor's invitation, I know in my heart I still had some dubious issues concerning religion.

Darkness Looms

Because about a year before, I had started going outback behind the house to smoke cigarettes. My sinister behavior was getting the best of me. I also noticed I wasn't the only one in the family having problems. While I was at school, someone called the school saying there was a bomb in one of the classes. The principal closed school early.

After the police and faculty investigation, it was determined my brother, Donald, was the culprit. He was detained and placed in a detention center for about three weeks.

Subsequently, my nefarious behavior continued spiraling downward. One day one of Daddy's whiskey customers came by to sample some whiskey before purchase. Daddy inadvertently left a pint mayonnaise jar half-full of whiskey on the living room coffee table. I proceeded with caution to take a little sip...Initially, it was too strong and I couldn't handle it. But, about five minutes later I was feeling euphoric. I went back and drank the remainder. I became wasted— staggering drunk, talking crazy out of my head. Daddy was going to whip me, until my sister, Sharon, told him I'd drank the whiskey on the coffee table. Fortunately I got by without a whipping.

Nevertheless I still persisted in my vices...As a vagabond, I became even more irresponsible. While at school, one day I decided to cut class and take a smoke. After about a half hour or so, I heard my name broadcast over the intercom— instructing me to report to the principal's office. Upon arriving at the principal's office, he proceeded to tell me I was seen smoking around side of the building by a faculty member. He therefor presented me an option: I could be suspended for a week, or stand up, turn around, place my hands up against the wall, while he administer five lashes on my behind with his leather strap. I thought for a few seconds, then agreed to his terms and accepted the whipping.

Consequently, I decided that smoking had to stop. I was busted...And that was it! When I arrived home, Mama told me: "Mr. Armstrong (an elderly neighborly white man) stopped by in need of someone to do some work around his house, and he would pay medium wage." Thus, I volunteered - working evenings after school and weekends. I kept the job for several years; things remained the same for about three years.

Arrested at Age Sixteen

It was August 1977; it was hot, and I was angry; I don't remember why I was angry, but I was on my last nerve. Anyway, I was sitting on the living room sofa running my finger through a pair of brass knuckles. (The brass knuckles belonged to my brother, Wilie Jr. Why they were laying around? I don't know.) My sister Dorothy came out from the kitchen with her dinner and sat next to me on the sofa to eat. She started smacking down her food like a dog eating slop. I asked her to stop smacking. She ignored me. I asked her again. She looked at me and said something in a smart aleck tone. I became fierce and snatched the glass of tea she was about to drink from her hand and broke it with the brass knuckles. I broke the glass to intimidate her; however, the glass shattered in mid-air inadvertently falling on her leg, cutting a gash just above her knee. She saw blood and started screaming for Mama.

When Mama heard Dorothy screaming she ran out from the kitchen to see what was the matter. When she too saw the blood, she panicked saying she was going tell Daddy and I was getting a whipping. I recalled the last whipping with a two foot water hose and said to myself: "No way." I ran and grabbed the shotgun from the wall-case and headed to the hills. I hid behind a dirt embankment about forty yards away. Daddy made it home about two hours after the incident. Mama did just as she said...I was waiting with gun in hand. I wasn't going to shoot my Daddy. In fact, I didn't even have any shells— I just wanted to intimidate him. He made an attempt to come get me, but when Mama told him I had the shotgun, he backed down and told my sister to call the police. When the police arrived, I surrendered and was escorted to the patrol vehicle and detained for about three weeks; I went before a judge and was sentenced to serve three months in a youth crisis center.

Whispers of Darkness

Showing up at the youth crisis center, I didn't know what to expect. The facility was a five bedroom house run by a middle age white couple. However, the set-up was inviting and hospitable. My fellow inmates were three white girls: Cindy, Nancy, and Cathy. Also, there were two other black guys, Darrel and Wayne; we had separate bunks. The girls slept across the hall. Darrel was asthmatic; however, Cathy and I believed Darrel faked an asthma attack at times to get attention. He loved being the center of attention. Oh— by the way, I forgot to mention that a few days after arriving at the youth detention center, I met a redhead white girl name, April— who was interested in being my friend. I was interested in her too. I especially liked her athletic ability on the volleyball court. I wasn't interested in establishing anything solid with either of the girls at the crisis center. I had a crush on April.

Upon my release my brother, Willie Jr., came to pick me up from the crisis center and escorted me home. When I returned home I apologized to my sister, Dorothy. Daddy didn't say anything; I guess he felt the time I spent in the crisis center was punishment enough. After a week or two of being around the house, I became bored with the same old humdrum. One night I was in bed and couldn't fall to sleep; an evil foreboding spirit entered my mind and whispered silently, saying: "Get up and break April out of jail." I got up and sat on side of the bed - it's like I was in a trance. It was around 10:30 or 11:00 P.M. I got dressed, eased out of the house, hopped on my bicycle and rode to Mrs. Armstrong house. Oh, incidentally, Mr. Armstrong had been dead about a year prior. Anyway, I eased up to her bedroom window. I heard her snoring like a bear in hibernation. I went to the garage to steal the vehicle, because I knew the driver-side door would be unlocked, and the keys were under the floor mat. After stealing the vehicle, I drove back to my family's house, parked about 60 or 70 yards down the street and walked stealthily in our house to borrow the shotgun. When I got back to the vehicle with gun-in-hand, I headed to the detention center and cased the place for about an hour— trying to build up the nerve to enter with the shotgun. But I couldn't muster enough nerve.

So, I got back into the vehicle, took the gun back home, and eased Mrs. Armstrong vehicle back into her garage.

Lost My Virginity at Seventeen

Several weeks had passed since I returned from the crisis center. Mama and Daddy asked me was I not going back to school? I said, "No...I've lost interest." Daddy said, "If you don't go back to school, then you need to find a job." So I decided to apply for a job at Anderson Tully's sawmill in Vicksbur - I was only sixteen years old; but I lied on the application, saying I was eighteen.

Following the interview, I was hired on the spot. I rode on the back of my Daddy's pickup, cause my other two brothers, Willie Jr. and Donald, rode in the cab; except when it rained, Daddy would squeeze me in next to him. Well, I finally had a real job making steady income. Daddy said to me if I saved enough money to make a down payment on a vehicle, he would purchase it for me in his name.

It took me about three months to save six hundred dollars for a down payment. Daddy kept his word...And we went to the dealership. I picked a nice clean 1977 Pontiac Grandprix, LJ edition. Sometimes after work I would get in my car and cruise through town and a few alleys checking out the honeys (girls). There was this fine, shapely young woman with a swag I couldn't resist walking next to the pavement. I cruised up beside her and said, "Hey baby!" She said, "Hey baby!" I said, "What's your name?" "Arletha," she said. I said, "Can I be your baby for real?" "Sure can!" she said. Thus, I got her number, called her, and we dated steady.

It's now November 1979, I was seventeen years old. Arletha was twenty-three years old, black woman - light brown complexion, with three kids, ages: three, five, and seven. Not long after we hooked up, I lost my virginity.

Whispers of Darkness Continue

One day while in the yard washing my vehicle, an evil foreboding spirit whispered silently in my mind: "Go rob Queen Hills Store." (Queen Hill's Store is a country store located on Hwy 22 five miles north of our house). At that moment I recalled Mama saying she would hum a spiritual hymn, and the foreboding evil spirit would leave. I did what I recalled Mama saying, and the evil spirit departed.

Accident

On September 4, 1980, 4:30 or 5:00 P.M., I was out in the yard cleaning up my car. My friend Kenny Singleton— who also worked at Anderson Tully's sawmill, walked up to me and said, "What's up?" I said, "Not much...I got a little weed, let's cruise a while." I concurred. But, before we entered my car, one of my weed customers drove up to buy sixty dollar worth of weed. I had the weed, but didn't have change for the hundred dollar bill which he had. Therefore my customer suggested, "Give me five minutes to run by my house and get change, and I'll meet you on the highway". I agreed. In about the space of three or four minutes, my brother Donald came across the yard walking toward the highway going to the store. I said, "I'm going your way, you want a ride?" "Yeah," he said.

We got into the car and headed up Highway 22. After traveling about two miles, I met my customer with the money change— $60.00. We made the exchange; I then made a U-turn at a fork in the road and headed back toward town. As I was cruising the speed limit around 50 or 55 miles per hour; I had passed my family's house about 75 yards when I was meeting a vehicle driven by my neighbor who lives across the street putting on her right hang signal...Suddenly a car come out to pass, we hit head on - collision! There we all were, Donald, Kenny, the other driver and me...They were all dead. My brother Willie Jr. ran up the highway to the scene and pulled us out of the vehicle before it caught fire. I was laying on the ground with my right lung collapsed, eight broken ribs, and passing in and out of consciousness from a concussion.

When the highway patrolman arrived on the scene, he was biased toward me because the driver in the other vehicle was a white man and dead. The patrolman was about to write me a traffic citation for passing on a (double-line) no passing zone. However, my neighbor who saw the whole incident came to my defense - citation avoided. I was carried to the university hospital in Jackson, Mississippi, treated, and released after two weeks.

Being released from the hospital was the beginning of a turning point in my life. The accident caused a big shift in my emotions and behavior. I just couldn't get past losing my brother, Donald, and friend, Kenney. I fell into a dark hole of deep depression. I went to visit my brother's grave site regularly, crying, angry and miserable. My pride was much too high to seek help. Nonetheless, I went back to church often hoping to hear a word of inspiration or something. But it was to no avail. In fact, the more I attended church, the depression and spirit of darkness prevailed to an even greater extent. About six months after the accident, I bought another car with the insurance settlement.

Whispers of Darkness Climax

Not being able to pull myself together, I quit working at Anderson Tully's sawmill and laid-up on Mama and Daddy. Arletha took the initiative and moved out of her mother's house into her own shotgun-style apartment house. I saw the move she made and decided to shack up with her. She didn't work, but lived off welfare and food stamps. As time went by, my depression eased up enough for me to go and find a job. It didn't take long. I went to a construction site in Clinton, Mississippi; the supervisor interviewed me and hired me on site.

Construction work never was steady work, because if the weather was bad I couldn't work. It was a Wednesday morning, and it had rained all day the day (Tuesday) before. I asked Arletha to fix me lunch for work; even though it had rained and the construction site was wet, I still needed to go out and find work.

As I cruised around looking for work, I couldn't find anything - it was just too wet. So, I pulled up to Mount Moriah Store— a country store south of Edwards. I went into the store to buy gas, but when I saw a young lady there alone, immediately the evil spirit raised up within me saying, "Rob her!" I went to purchase a pack of chewing gum, and when the saleswoman opened the cash register, I reached behind the counter, forcefully took her money and ran out of the store. While running towards the car, I heard something like fireworks. I looked back and saw the sales woman with a gun shooting at me; I kept running down the highway leaving the vehicle. When I ran about 60 yards - realizing I had nowhere to go; I turned around and surrendered - hands in the air. She then said, "Put the damn money on the ground and get the hell out of here." Doing as she instructed, I got into my car and drove to my brother's (Willie Jr.) house to lay-low a few hours. Willie Jr. wasn't home from work. Nevertheless I needed to hide out just in case the saleswoman called the police. I left my car parked in Willie Jr.'s driveway with the key in the ignition, and walked through a pathway in the woods to Daddy's house.

Daddy made it home about 45 minutes later, and started unloading firewood from his

64

pickup truck. I went to him for the first time with a problem telling him I just robbed Mt. Moriah Store. But before he could say anything my brother Charles drove up to tell me he was driving pass Stuckey's Restaurant and the police flagged him over, questioning him of my whereabouts. He suggested we go down to Stuckey's to resolve the matter. I said, "Okay."

The police started asking me questions of my whereabouts around the time Mount Moriah Store was robbed, and where was my car? I perceived the police weren't sure I was the culprit because the saleswoman gave them the wrong description of the vehicle. So I lied and said, "Arletha has my car in Jackson shopping." They believed me, and were about to let me go. However, it was about that same time my brother Willie Jr. drove up in my car; perhaps thinking I needed a ride home. The officer that knew me knew my car too. He asked to have a look in my trunk. I opened the truck. He spotted the striped overall I was wearing doing the robbery according to the saleswoman's description. I was busted!

Arrested (Strong-armed Robbery)

On November 5, 1981, I was arrested and charged with strong-armed robbery of Mount Moriah Store in Edwards. I was nineteen years old, facing a fifteen year sentence. It was after the finger printing and mug-shot that I really began to feel the seriousness of my crime. After booking (finger printing and mug-shots) I was placed in a holding cell awaiting bond. While awaiting release - about five days - I really tried to make sense of this ordeal, but I just couldn't understand the evil darkness in my heart. Nevertheless. I made bond and was escorted home by Mama and Arletha.

Although I was home, I was still facing a fifteen year prison sentence. Being fresh out of jail, seems I should have learned my lesson - but no, I was still depressed from the accident and angry for not having answers to the evil darkness within. I kept going back to church every Sunday and I would do well until around Wednesday. The more I sat my mind to do good, evil would intensify...Additionally, I was now beginning the worry about the robbery charge. It had gotten to the point I was hurting and miserable every single day...I just wanted to end it all.

Sexual Assault

It was the month of February 1982; I was living with Arletha. I became fed-up with the evil darkness within and decided to no longer fight with my emotions; instead I would give in to them. I told Arletha I was going out for a while and have a few drinks. I got into my car and drove to the liquor store and purchased a fifth of whiskey. As soon as I returned to the car, I broke the seal and turn the bottle upside down in my mouth drinking about one half pint straight - nonstop.

After guzzling the straight whisky, I was ready for anything the Spirit of Darkness would bring. Thus, I started up the car and began cruising down highway 22; it was about 10:30 P.M. I was passing by Pattie Bradley's house when I saw her half-dressed before turning off the light to her bedroom. The evil spirit of darkness raised-up within me immediately! Parking my car on a gravel road nearby - about 50 yards away from Pattie's house; I walked up and knocked on the door. Upon seeing me, and knowing who I was, she opened the door. I then forced myself upon her sexually.

Serving Hard Time

On February 1982, I was twenty years old, and also arrested for Sexual Battery of Pattie D. Bradley. This was my second felony; I knew that I would be gone a long time. However, Arletha came to my defense and talked with Pattie Bradley...She dropped the charges. Notwithstanding, the District Attorney picked up the case and offered a deal of two years concurrent with the 10 year sentence for the strong-armed robbery; I accepted the deal and remained there in the county jail nine months.

As of November 1982, I was transferred to the Mississippi State Penitentiary to serve the remainder of my ten year sentence.

CLIFTON NICKENS
#186266

Clifton Nickens was raised in a small farming community on the outskirts of Hammond, Louisiana. He has been married for 20 years and he worked as a field engineer in the chemical industry for 17 years until his arrest in February, 2013. He is currently serving a twelve year sentence for statutory rape.

One Son's Story

Clifton Nickens

In the year of our Lord 1961, on the 8th day of the month of January, a son, Clifton Ray Nickens, was born to Perkins Melvin and Minnie Jane Nickens Jr. at Seventh Ward General Hospital in Hammond, Louisiana. It was told to me by my parents that the day of my birth, was cold, windy, lightning and rainy; and that I was born around 2:00 A.M., in the early hours of the morning.

Our home was located in the small, rural farming community of Pumpkin Center, Louisiana. The community is located along Interstate 55, approximately four miles west of the city of Hammond, Louisiana. My grandfather had moved to the area in 1903, before the community had a name of its own. My grandfather purchased 300 acres of property on which he would raise my father, three more sons and two daughters. My grandfather then proceeded to make a living as a woodsman, cattle farmer, and vegetable farmer.

My mother was born in Mt. Herman, Mississippi, to parents who were cotton sharecropping farmers. My mother's mother died in a coal oil stove explosion when my mother was 12 years old. My mother, her three brothers, and three sisters were then given by their father to a foster care home. My step-grandfather, Clyde Starkey, adopted my mother, all her brothers, sisters, and moved them to his farm in Pumpkin Center, Louisiana. It would be here that my mother would be raised, would eventually meet my father, and be married to him.

My father, a carpenter and vegetable and cattle farmer along with my grandfather, closed an acre of my grandfather's property to build us a home. My father built us a small, cozy, 36' long, 18' wide, one room, shotgun house in which to live. The house had a tin roof 1 x 12 pine board siding, with a heavy, asphalt, roll roofing over the wood siding. The house had two doors, one in the front, and one directly opposite of it in the rear of the house. The house had five windows, two on each long-side of the house, one of those was over the kitchen sink and one window in the front of the house on the left side of the front door. The interior of the house was an open room, no interior walls or partitions. Upon entering the front door, there were two double beds to the left, two upright dressers with drawers, and a hanging rod for our clothes, on the right side wall of the room. Also on this right side wall, past the window, was my mother's white, metal china cabinet for our bowls, plates, cups, and utensils. On the left wall, past the beds, there was a multicolored metal table, with four metal cushioned seat chairs. Beyond the table was a white, metal double sink unit, with drawers, and four doors with shelves for pots, pans, and the food. The rear wall had a white stove and refrigerator against it, also on the left side of the rear door.

Beside the kitchen sink there was no indoor plumbing, no commode, bathtub or laundry. The outhouse toilet was located out the rear door of the house, to the left, about 100' away. We had a pump, wash, and storage shed about 50' directly behind the house. The shed housed my mother's white washing machine, with its swing away ringer head for pressing the water out of the wet clothes. It also stored our #3, metal, galvanized wash tub, in which we took our baths. In the spring, summer, and early fall, when there was a lot of sunshine, the tub was filled and left to heat in the sun.

We were then given baths, in the early evenings, before the sun set. In the winter, we would heat water on the stove, fill the tub, and take our baths inside.

It would be here that my father and mother would choose to raise my two sisters and I. One of my sisters, Vanessa, is three years older than I, and my other sister, Ramona, is three years younger than I. I at this time of my life am four years old, kind of tall for my age, medium build, blackish brown hair, with dark brown eyes. I was, I reckon to say, as most boys my age, who were being raised in the country, full of energy, exploring, curious, and at times rambunctious. I was a lover of the outdoors; one of my favorite places to play and explore, especially in the summertime, was under the house. Our house was about 2 ½ feet above the ground, with plenty of cool shade and dirt to play in. It was here that I would hide from my sisters, playing with my dump truck, motor grader, army jeep and army men. All the time patiently waiting for my sisters and mother, so that I could reach, grab their legs, scream loud and scare them.

The front yard, guarded by a net wire fence, bordered the Perkins Nickens Sr. gravel road, which had been named after my grandfather. There were along this net wire fence, huge, virgin pine trees of massive size and 100' tall. On this gravel road, one day a week, would come one of my four year old boyish enjoyments. It was my Uncle Vincent, working for the parish, grading the gravel roads, on the big, yellow, loud motor grader. He would always stop in front of our house, wave and holler to me as I stood behind and peering through the squares of the net fence. I was wide eyed, waving back vigorously, with a huge smile upon my face. I could hear the front door of the house creak open, behind me, as my uncle stepped down from the machine. It was my mother, coming out of the house, with a cup of coffee in her hand. The coffee cup was given to my uncle, as he entered the yard and greetings were made between him and my mother. I would wait nervously beside my mother, as if I had ants in my pants for the joy I knew was coming. Finally, after what seemed like a lifetime, my uncle would say, "Well, I reckon I better get back to work, thanks for the coffee you all," and begin to walk off. My heart, would stop for a moment - had he forgotten? - and just then he would turn and say, "Well Clifton are you coming or not." My heart would start up again wildly, as I looked up at my mother for approval and she would say, "Well I reckon you can ride; but please be careful." I would take off like a young stallion, yelling, jumping, and running towards the big, yellow, motor grader.

The time is around July or August of 1966; I am five years old. My father has not been to work for the past three or four days, because it has been raining a lot and very stormy. My father and mother are packing our clothes in a suitcase; my sisters and I are being bundled up and packed one by one through the pouring rain into the car outside. My parents finish loading everything and we drive down the 3/8 mile lane,

70

beside our house, to my grandfather's house at the rear of the farm. We, along with our suitcases, are brought upon the porch and into my grandfather's house.

My grandfather's house is on a concrete slab, with brick siding, and a shingle roof. It is "L" shaped with front, rear and side porches. My whole family is here, my uncles, aunts and my only cousin at this time, Kearney, a boy baby of one year old. I hear a lot of talk about the bad weather and something they are calling a hurricane. I don't know what a hurricane is; but it has everyone looking and talking worriedly. My father says it is going to hit us by this afternoon. The women are busy cooking, keeping coffee made for everyone, and making bed pallets on the floor for everyone to sleep on. I can begin to hear the wind howling and screaming as it blows through the trees and around the buildings on my grandfather's farm. It is turning darker outside, as I step out the door onto the porch and in between my father and grandfather. My father places his hand upon my head gently, as they stare down the lane at our house. I can hear them talking about our house and whether it will be able to withstand the storm. The wind and rain is so strong now that my father and grandfather grab me and back up against the brick wall of the porch. The rain is being driving sideways by the howling, screaming wind and is hitting the house like rocks. The sound of the storm is almost deafening to me as I bury myself into the blue jeans of my father's leg.

I hear my grandfather say, "There it goes; she's not going to be able to take much more on. She's going to come apart." I look up from my blue jean protection to see the tin roof of our house being torn apart by the howling, sheer, driving winds and rain. My father at this point tells me to go back inside with my mother and sisters. We are all fed and put to bed for the night on our thick, quilt laden pallets. I awake in the morning to the smell of coffee, biscuits, bacon and eggs being cooked for everyone to eat breakfast. I look for my father and mother, whom I couldn't find inside. I opened the door to the porch to find everyone outside, drinking morning coffee, and smoking cigarettes. I was saddened immediately by the tears that were flowing down my mother's cheeks and the somber look on my father's face. I instantly went to my mother, who grabbed me, pulled me into her bosom and said, "Thank God that none of us or our children are hurt." I begin to be filled with emotion, tears swelling up in my eyes, and overflowing onto my cheeks as I squeezed my mother tightly.

My father buys a house and three acres of land. The new house is 3 ¼ miles away from my grandfather's farm at the north end of the community. The hurricane had destroyed our home and my father decided not to rebuild it. The new house is rectangular, as our old house was. However, it has a front porch, a separate kitchen, separate living room, two bedrooms and a bathroom. We have an indoor commode, lavatory, bathtub, and all have hot water in the faucets. Maybe moving isn't so bad, maybe good things can come from bad things! But I still miss our old house and grandfather's farm. Oh, no, what about my weekly ride with Uncle Vincent, on the big yellow, noisy, motor grader? Our new home is on a gravel road; but it is a dead end and does he come up here to work? Well, to my surprise, Uncle Vincent did work on our road, my rides continued as usual, and I was learning to adjust to our new farm.

The next two years of me being seven and eight years old were filled with much growing, maturing, exploring, responsibilities and work. My 7th year of age would see me begin school at Hammond Elementary School. There were none of my cousins here; they all went to Ponchatoula schools, where the rest of the community went except for the northern part, which went to Hammond. I began to explore the surrounding woods, creeks, ponds, and the Natalbany River, which ran ¼ mile behind our house. I became an avid runner, running through the wood trails, along the creek banks and on the sand bars of the river. It was in the first and second grades that I discovered, and became passionate about, running track. I was the boy to beat at all the track meets in the 50 and 100 yard race. I won many trophies, ribbons and awards. I also excelled in long jump, short jump, and the relay. I would go on to compete until my 4th grade year.

My father and I started clearing trees from the land to make fields for planting and grass plots for grazing. He would cut down the big oak and pine trees, de-limb them, then I would drag and stack them on the stumps to burn. It was my mother, sisters, and my job to keep the pines stacked and burning. We were also given the job of clearing the perimeter fencing of all trees, brush, and shrubs. We were repairing the fence to prepare for the calves that father would put on the grass plots.

My 8th year found me helping building hog pens for three female pigs, who we named after my mother's three sisters: Rosie, Barbara and Laura. They were not to be used for breeding, but for slaughtering, which we would all do as a family. We built new chicken pens, with roosts and laying boxes for about 30 chickens. We raised chicks and killed chickens for our winter food supply. We spent the early spring clearing, plowing and planting our vegetable garden. We spent the summer months picking vegetables, sitting under the huge live oak trees in the backyard, and shelling peas, beans and shucking corn. On large wooden tables we would wash, sort, clean, cook, can in jars and store in the canning shed everything we had harvested that summer. It wasn't always work; my father, mother, sisters and I would take a big watermelon to the river. We would bury the watermelon in the cold sandy water and it would chill while we swam and played.

Dad would then take the watermelon, cut it open; oh how red, juicy it would be, with that sweet wonderful smell! We all sitting waist deep in the cool, clear, running water would eat our watermelon laughing and having fun.

In 1970, I turned 9 years old and the year began with me going to the doctor for my hearing. My teachers, along with my parents had discovered that I was hearing impaired. It would take many trips to the doctor, much school missed and much expense to my parents, before they found out that I had lost the coverings off of my eardrums. It had been four years earlier, when I had the measles with a high fever for several days and severe ear infections. It was the combination of all the illnesses that ruptured my ears and caused my hearing loss. It would be from nine years old, until I was fifteen years old, that I would undergo five major ear operations. This would put an end to my normal boy childhood, my swimming, my running, my friends; all fun activities stopped. The operations would require that I have my head shaved, my ears kept dry at all times, including no excessive sweating. No loud noises, no sudden jars like running, jumping, no swimming. No hollering, no sneezing, no sucking through straws, no holding your nose, etc. I felt like my life had just been taken away from me and I should just stay shut up inside or walk gently around outside, with my hands in my pocket.

If having my head shaved in preparation for the surgery and being ridiculed by all the children at school wasn't bad enough, it was being taken into an operating room on a stretcher, a wire mask with cotton gauze on it being placed over my mouth, and ether being hand poured on it. The ether was overpowering, I was being told by the nurse to count backwards, and all the time struggling to breathe until I lost consciousness. The surgeries were all twelve hours long, with a full day in the recovery room, before being moved to a room for a couple of days and finally released back home. I would spend a week at home, always having a large 7" x 7" x 2" thick bun over my ear and a head band. I had to attend school like this, no playing, no P.E., just standing around like a foul smelling, sore wrapped, bald headed reject. I wanted to crawl into a hole and never come out of it again. I became even more discouraged, depressed, and hopeless when I went back to the doctor. He removed the smelly bandage, cleaned, checked my stitches that were from my sideburn into my lower rear part of my ear and horribly, unbearably said that the operation was a failure. The skin grafts that he had placed inside my ear didn't stay attached; they tore. I wanted to run out of the office screaming, "No, not again, I can't take it anymore."

However, it was not my decision, I was only a child and my parents, along with the doctor, decided to try the operation again. Well, for my right ear I had three surgeries and for my left ear I had two surgeries of which none were successful. It was finally ended when I was 15 years old. I explained to my parents that I was willing to live with my impairment, I didn't want to go through any more surgeries; and they agreed. It was a breath of fresh air to my soul, like coming out of a tight, musky, damp, dark tunnel, and breaking forth into the light, life and fresh air again.

It was the Christmas of my 10th year of age that brought a breath of fresh air to my bewildering life that had begun as a 9 year old child. My family always looked forward to Christmas, especially my mother, who would cook for a week prior to Christmas Day. She was prepared for everyone that would come by, beginning the night of Christmas Eve until the night of Christmas dinner and beyond. However, two days before Christmas, after supper my father gathered us all in the living room to talk to us. My father, explained that my mother's oldest sister and her husband, Uncle Kiddeboo, Aunt Loraine Anthony and their three boys and four girls were in a very poor way. My father asked us all to give our presents, plus extra they had bought, and all the food Mom had prepared to them. He said they didn't know we were coming and that Christmas morning we would load everything into the old blue Falcon station wagon and surprise them.

Uncle Kiddeboo was a tenant dairy farmer for a large dairy farm in Greensburg, Louisiana. It was about 30 or 40 miles north of where we lived. It was about 4:00 A.M., Christmas morning, and we all got out of bed, loaded all the presents and food into the station wagon and took off. We were all so excited, jolly, we sang songs and talked all the way there. We arrived at the home about an hour after daylight. My father, instead of knocking on the front door, took handfuls of large gravel rocks from the driveway and threw them continually upon the tin roof. It didn't take but a moment for us to hear running and hollering in the house. My uncle came to the front door. It swung open; there he was no shoes, no socks, no shirt, blue jeans barely on, hair all out of place, a week's old beard on his face, a shotgun in his hand and hollering, "Who in the hell is that rocking my roof, I'll shoot your ass."

My father yelled, "Kiddeboo, man you ain't gonna shoot nobody, you know that ole gun don't work." He said, "Perk, Perk, is that you, man come on in, hey Lorraine, it's Perk, Minnie, and the kids, put on some coffee, we got company." We unloaded the station wagon, took all the presents and food inside and went through greetings for what seemed like an hour. My uncle, my aunt and all my cousins were speechless and most were crying as they received all we had brought to them. It was a wonderful day, we helped milk and played with all the calves, goats, and chickens all day. It had been the best Christmas that me and my family ever had. It brought our two families closer together than we ever had been before. Love is an amazing attribute that can't be outdone, nor does the memory of it fade away. This was an awesome end to the 10th year of my life. A year that had its trials, hardships, and at times failures; but the end mightily outweighs the means.

However, as with seasons, so are our lives; the 11th year of my life would bring new burdens, trials, sadness and sorrow for me, my family, and the Anthony's.

GERGORY FRAZIER
#1844000

Gregory Frazier is a Parchman inmate serving a 20 year sentence for aggravated assault.

Snake Creek

Gregory Frazier

The Toddler Years

I.

I lived the first couple of years of my life in Snake Creek. Snake Creek was an area of land with a long twisting creek running through it. The land was located in between Cleveland, Mississippi and Pace, Mississippi in the part of Mississippi known as The Delta.

There were only a few houses on Snake Creek. These houses were occupied by other members of my family.

The houses were old unpainted wooden framed homes that were built in a style called Shotgun.

All the rooms in a Shotgun house are in a straight line. Such as, there is a porch with the front entrance to the main part of the house located at the back of the porch. At the rear of the living room was a door that led to a bedroom with two doors. One led to the kitchen and the other one to a room that was used as a toilet. At the rear of the kitchen was a door that led to another bedroom, and at the rear of that bedroom was another door that led to another bedroom.

Snake Creek was very rough terrain, covered by dirt, small pebbles, and surrounded by thick woods.

There was a pathway that led from our house down to the creek where Mom would go fishing. I can remember Mom walking down the pathway with her large straw hat on, and carrying her long tan cane poles in her hand. My brother was pulling me in a small metal red wagon. Every time he would start to pull the wagon I would yell. The vibration of the wagon being pulled across the rough terrain would painfully irritate my ears. It was horrifying for me, and at my young age I didn't know what was happening, but every time the wagon would start to move I would start to yell. At some point someone must have figured out why I was yelling, because my brother, who is 15 years older than me, lifted me up out the wagon and carried me the rest of the way on his shoulders.

II.

Summer days in the Mississippi Delta are extremely hot and humid. On this particular day, the sun was even more cruel and unapologetic. Its fierce rays gave our little Shotgun house a vicious beating.

In places where the ground had started to crack from the intense heat it appeared to me that the earth was trying to provide the Shotgun a hiding place from the brutal sun, until the rain came to its rescue. The heat waves that came from the pavement made it appear that Highway 8 West was mourning the abuse of the Little Shotgun at the hands of the relentless sun. In simpler words, "It was too damn hot."

I was sitting in my play pen. It was a four by four feet wooden framed pen surrounded by four feet tall wooden bars that were spaced only far enough for a toddler my size to get his head stuck in between them. The play pen was no less than a four by four prison cell for toddlers.

I wasn't wearing anything but a white cloth diaper that clung to my sweaty little bottom. The extreme heat and the lack of any kind of air circulation made the diaper feel like an overcoat. I was hot and agitated, so out of frustration I took off the diaper and flung it over the bars. I then flung the powder blue pacifier over the bars. Finally I flung the matching blue plastic bottle over the bars.

I laid back in the pen and gave a deep sigh. I grabbed the yellow plastic baby bottle, the only thing that I hadn't thrown out of the pen, and popped its tan rubber nipple in my mouth. As soon as it was registered to my taste buds that it was milk and not apple juice in the bottle, I spit the milk and nipple out, all in one motion.

Dang!

I had flung the wrong bottle out of the pen!

I had intended to throw the milk bottle out, but instead I had thrown my beloved apple juice bottle over the bars.

I became as irate as a toddler was allowed to become. "It was too hot for milk! What kind of kid don't know the difference between his milk bottle and his juice bottle! A stupid kid like me. That's who!"

The bottle had landed about three feet from the play pen.

I got down on my stomach and stuck my hand in between the bars in an attempt to retrieve the juice bottle. My arm was not long enough to reach it, but I was determined to retrieve my juice bottle.

I reasoned that if I could get my head between the bars that I may be able to reach the bottle. So I went for it.

I grabbed a hold on two of the bars and pulled my body as hard as I could towards them. This caused my head to move between the bars, but I still couldn't reach my juice bottle. I had to try something else. I tried to pull my head back through the bars.

"Uh Oh!"

This was not good. My head was stuck between the bars.

I felt something warm trickled out of my nose and dropped to the floor just beneath where my head was hanging out of the pen. The fluid rapidly started to flow at a more constant pace. This couldn't be a good thing. I'd learned when stuff came out of my body it needed an adult's attention.

I hadn't yet learned to speak adult language, but I knew if I cried someone would usually pay attention to me. However I didn't want to cry. I reasoned that I could handle this on my own.

I needed to figure out what the stuff was that was coming out of my nose, and how to stop it. I had to figure out how to get my head out of the bars and how to get my juice bottle.
My sister Zet is seventeen years older than I am. She'd taught me many things, so I went through the motion of trying to remember what stuff she said came out what places of my body.

Shit? No. This was not shit. Shit was either brown, yellow, or green. Most, but not all the time, it was shaped in lumpy balls. It was really stinking and it came from the hole in the bottom of my body that Zet called my "boo-boo". This definitely wasn't shit!

Piss? No. It was not piss either. Piss was a yellow liquid that came out of the hose in the front of my body that Zet called my "pee-pee". Piss burned like hell. Nope. This was not piss.

Snot? Maybe. Snot was thick slimy yellow stuff that came out of what Zet called my nose. It was my nose that the stuff was coming out of, but it was the wrong color. This was not snot.

It was something familiar about this liquid. I had seen it before. Then I remembered. It was called blood, and that's what the hogs did just before they died after my brothers would shoot them in between the eyes with the old rifle.

I quickly reasoned that I was going to die like the hogs, because I sure was bleeding like one. I panicked and tried to cry as I'd learned to do when I wanted the attention of an adult, but for reasons I can't explain I yelled, "Shit!"

Everyone in the house came running to my rescue. I guess I handled the situation like an adult when they got in trouble. I panicked and cursed.

III.

At some point the man who owned Snake Creek died. His son inherited the land and ordered all the occupants of Snake Creek to vacate the land.

Gone was the sound of the flowing creek and the night creatures that formed its orchestra. Gone was the sight of the large trees that danced to the beats of the spring winds. Gone was the serenity of the country sky. Gone were our livestock and freshly grown vegetables. Gone was that innocent little boy who had gotten his head stuck in between the play pen bars. All that remained were the wonderful memories of my life on the creek.

Town: The Teen Years

IV.

We moved to Cleveland, Mississippi. A place that we referred to only as "Town".

Town life was not kind to me and my family. Moving from Snake Creek to Town was like falling from a mountain top and landing on quicksand. To say that we didn't adjust well would be the understatement of the millennium. We went from abundance to poverty in one swift motion.

Poverty travels with an entourage including, but not limited to: Tragedy, Crime, Shame, Pain and Death. All of which I have gotten to know on a first name basis.

My mom was fifty years old when she had me, therefore all of my siblings were grown and had children of their own when I was born.

My oldest brother killed a man during a gambling dispute. To avoid arrest he left town. His wife, along with my two older twin sisters, Red and Black, robbed and killed a local business owner. As a result, the three of them were sentenced to prison for manslaughter. That left my mom to raise me, my six nephews, and my niece, and she had to do this on the minimum wage income of a maid, food stamps, and welfare.

The total income was only a fraction of what it took to raise eight children. The stamps were issued only once a month, and Mom always had to sell some of them to the bootleg preacher for half their face value, to get cash to help pay some of the utilities and the rent on the many condemned houses that we were constantly moving into, because we just couldn't afford any better.

As a result of Mom selling the food stamps we were always short on food. In fact, we were always short on something! Short on toilet paper. Short on soap. Short on detergent. Short on utilities. Short on clothes and sometimes even short on life. But we were never short on love.

V.

The winter of 1979 was one of the coldest on record for the Mississippi Delta. Unfortunately, we lived at 501 Ruby Street, Cleveland, Mississippi.

The house had a single coat of old yellow dingy paint that was peeling away. It was a two bedroom, boxed shaped, wooden framed structure. The walls and ceiling were not insulated; the roof had holes in it the size of pennies; the exterior doors had at least a one inch space in between them and their seals, and we had to stuff many of the windows with cardboards and old rags, because of missing window panes.

The gas company refused to turn the gas on at 501 Ruby Street, because the old metal gas lines had corroded and leaked. Therefore, the only source of heat that we had was two small electrical heaters and an electrical hot plate that we also used to cook on.

Old man winter pimp slapped the small heaters around like a drunken abusive stepfather slaps his wife and stepson around. Likewise our bodies shivered and ached from his heavy hand. We all had on several layers of clothes. We cuddled up close together and wrapped ourselves in blankets and homemade quilts that Mom had made when we lived on the creek, but we could still feel the lashing old man winter dealt to us.

My nephew, Toby, was the baby of the bunch. He was only two years old. He had developed a very rough, dry cough. He was no longer breathing, but rather gasping for air. His little frail body was burning with fever, and it was pouring with sweat.

Mom was still at work. We knew that this was no ordinary cold virus that would just go away on its own. We had to get the baby to the doctor.

We didn't have a telephone, but there was one in the corner store across the street from our house.

I reached under the top bunk mattress and retrieved the two .38 revolvers Mom had kept from our days on the creek. I took one and stuffed in my jeans and pulled my long plaid short over it. I gave the other one to my nephew, Kick, who was two years older than me. "Me and Kick are going to the Corner Store to call Mom and an ambulance," I announced to the others.

I had armed us because the store owner didn't like my nephews, because he had caught them stealing on several occasions. However, he and I got along well. I didn't know if he would let me use his phone or not. All I knew was that I was willing to do whatever it took for me to call an ambulance and my mom. The calls were necessary if we had to do something that could be construed as evil to make those calls, then it would be a necessary evil.

Mr. Wong, the store's owner, ran the store with his wife.

As soon as Kick and I entered the store Mr. Wong's eyes locked on us suspiciously.

There were no other customers in the store. Mr. Wong was standing at the counter. As I walked up to the counter Mr. Wong appeared as if he was about to say something, but I interrupted him before he could get any words out.

Mr. Wong was a short, small framed oriental man in his mid-fifties. He didn't speak good English, but he spoke it well enough to communicate.

"Mr. Wong, my youngest nephew is very sick. May I please use your phone to call an ambulance and my mom?" I asked as politely as I could.
"You talk about little one?" He asked in his best English.

"Yes," I replied.

"No problem." He replied back as he passed me the phone from behind the counter.

After I had made the calls I assured Mr. Wong that my nephews wouldn't steal from him again.

Toby died on his way to the hospital from pneumonia complications. His death set in motion many necessary evils. My nephews and I had gotten short on tolerance.

S. K. SHADDIX
#179638

S. K. Shaddix is a screen writer from California. He is currently serving a two year sentence for a concealed weapon charge.

Highlights of My Youth: Part 1

S. K. Shaddix

The Cop in the Car and the Ride in the Rain

The first time I got in the back of a police car I was only nine years old. It would become a familiar experience as I grew older, but I didn't know it then.

I had just left the Long Beach, MS Public Library, and my arms were filled with a heavy load of books. The library was my favorite place and my first place to go to after school, which was right across the street.

When the librarian noticed that I'd become bored with the children's section she took my hand and led me to the aisles of the adult books. "Let me know if you find anything you like," she told me. I like the first book I saw, "The Warren Commission Report," and with it I walked to a table. The book was bigger and so were the chairs, and sitting there I felt bigger too. (I didn't understand very much about that book, but one thing was crystal-clear. There's no such thing as a 'Magic Bullet.' I knew this first hand from digging them up in Virginia. Bullets went into a gun in a pristine condition, and when they came out they were marked and disfigured. I'd seen it countless times, and my collection of them was prized and special to me.)

My arms are loaded with books and I'm on my way back home. A bit late, but my mom was used to it. "Wait a minute, Mom," I often told her.

The morning had begun warm and sunny, so I'd boarded the school bus that morning without a jacket or umbrella. The sun was still out when I went into the library, but when I came out it had grown dark and cloudy. That didn't concern me because I had only a few blocks to go until I made it home. I almost made it.

I was coming up to the railroad tracks that ran parallel to the Gulf of Mexico, when the sky suddenly erupted with a downpour of rain, thunder and lightning. That didn't bother me. I liked it. It was my books that I was concerned about. I'm a bookworm. I love books. Books fare poorly in the rain. I hunched over them as a parent would a child, and I quickened my pace. I'd reached the tracks when I heard a voice call out beside me, "Son! Hey there! Come over here!" It was a police man. "Yes, sir!" I said. "Where are you going, son?!" he said through the open passenger window of his patrol car. "Going home, sir. I live four blocks over on Nicholson." The rain fell even heavier now, and I wanted to be on my way. However, my father was a Navy Chief, Construction Battalion, and I was raised to respect my elders, which at my age was most everyone.

"Nicholson, huh? That's not far. You want a ride? Hop in. I'll give you a ride."

Immediately my desire to move on dissipated. A ride in a police car was irresistible, and impossible to refuse. I wouldn't do so even if the day were sunny and bright. I could tell all my friends about this one.

"Yes, sir!! I exclaimed. "Uh, um, um..." He opened the front door for me and said, "Get in!" "Uh... can I ride in the back?" I asked quietly. He gave me a gentle smile. "Sure. Hop in the back. Just hurry up!" I jumped in the back before he could change his mind, congratulating myself for even asking. I almost didn't. I looked around me. The only difference I could see was the metal screen that divided the car's interior between the front seats and the back. He looked at me through the screen. "Be there in a minute." We stopped at the red light, the only one in Long Beach, and another daring request came to mind. Emboldened by my previous success, I blurted out, "Can you turn on the siren?" He barked out a loud laugh and with a big smile said, "We can do that." We, he said. We. That makes us a team! When the light turned green, he flipped a switch and I heard it scream. Cool, so cool, so very, very cool. The siren was loud, but not so loud as it sounded on the street. It stayed with us, though, and didn't rise and fall away in sound. "This is way better than the roller-coaster!" I cried out, and he answered with that barking laugh again.

We turned on my street and I knew it was over. The ride of my life. "Wait till I tell Mom!" I thought, "I can't wait!"

I didn't have to wait long. I saw her getting into her car as we pulled up, and the siren startled her into dropping her keys. She rushed to the police car with a terrified look on her face. "Is he ok?! Oh, my God please tell me he's..." "Yes ma'am," the officer told her. "I gave him a ride because of the rain." She looked in the front seat. "Where is he" You said you..." "Ma'am. He's ok. He's in the back." "Whaa.. Why?! What's he done?" My mother was not a calm woman, by nature. I reached out to the door for the handle, spilling books onto the floorboard. I couldn't find the handle. Maybe it was broken. "Hey, mister. I can't open the door. How do..." Once again, that bark, and this one louder and longer than before. "Hold on, son." I heard a loud click. He got out of the car and came around the back to my door and opened it, smiling all the while.

"Thank you, mister!" I got out with my armful of books, and ran into my house. My first ride in a police car was over.

There would be many more rides to come in my life. None of them would have so happy an ending.

JAMIE FIELDS
#167999

Jamie Fields is a Parchman inmate serving a 10 year sentence for possession of cocaine with the intent to distribute.

The Year I Remember

Jamie Fields

I remember when I was going to school. I used to love having spelling bees and math quizzes because we were always timed. I remember those days. I came in first place in Spelling. Spelling was one of my best subjects that year. I remember my teacher giving us popcorn and a Sprite for winning. My teacher was so proud of me being a part of those events, she gave me $5.00 also. I couldn't believe that she was giving me $5.00 for winning those events.

I started going to more events after I won those events. I even tried computer quizzes, but I never won. I continued to attend even though I didn't win and I never gave up. I remember this female in my computer class. This female was very skilled when it came down to computers, so I asked her to give me lessons on the computers. After a few weeks, I went back to the computer class to re-enter the event that I'd lost weeks ago and came in second place. I was fine coming in 2nd place, but my computer teacher said I could do better which I knew I could, so we decided to carry out the computer lessons and as time went by, I got even better. I just knew that when I went to that computer event again, that I would be number one. I knew that I would have to study really hard to win the number one spot, so I didn't go back until I beat that person's record who won last time. The final event, I went to the computer event and when I got there I saw my computer teacher, she was there to cheer me on. I felt like I owed her this time and that I was going to try like hell to win this time. Well they finally decided to start the class. I usually took 45 minutes to complete the test. This time it only took me 35 minutes, so when they came on the intercom and said Jamie Fields was the winner, I was so excited that I hugged my teacher and told her thanks for helping me win the computer class. I knew then that you could do anything if you would just believe in the Lord and also keep studying. Ever since that day I knew if you put effort in what you are doing you will succeed. I loved trying things people said I couldn't do so I could prove them wrong. That day I walked around with a big smile on my face with the prize in my hand showing it off, everyone started clapping for me saying I done a great job. When they told me that, I told everyone what I was taught all my life and I say: never quit school and never give up. School is very important, we all need an education. After I decided that I was going to continue to go to school. I was wrong, they'd kicked me out because of me and another guy fighting. The other guy's name was Mike. Mike hit me in the face with a book, so I hit him in the face with my fist without asking who done it and what for. So both of us were throwing some hellish blows. I mean we were going tick for tack. Until all of the sudden I was the only one swinging. I start to wonder why there wasn't any more blows thrown from Mike. Mike was knocked out. He was on the ground folded up looking like he saw a ghost or something. At that time, I didn't know what was my next move because he'd pushed me to the point that I didn't know when to quit because I always had a problem with my temper. Once I get started it was always hard for me to control my attitude. I made a bad choice because they ended up calling both of us to the office to hear both of our sides. He told them his side of the story first, then I went in the office second after he came out. Before I could get my side of the story out, he told me that I would be expelled from school for the rest of the year and that I had to attend another school for my actions and that I would have to be there for two years. Well I started going to school only for a while, until I saw every time something would happen they would always bring my name up even if I wasn't there. I knew then that they really didn't want me there by the things they would say and do. I started to wonder why I was still at this school when there was nothing but drama there. So I slowly began to skip school. As I was skipping school, I began to get lazy, I lost interest so I stopped going. When I stopped the principal called my house to see why I wasn't at school. My mother asked me what was going on and why was the principal calling our house. When I explained why, she couldn't believe the words that were coming out my mouth. I told her I couldn't continue to go to that school because they were always pointing at me.

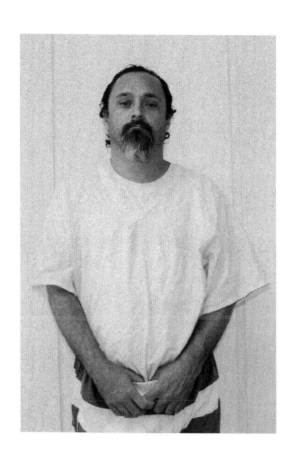

MELVIN MILES
#185678

Melvin Miles was raised in Mobile, Alabama. He is an adventurer who has worked on many fishing vessels around the country. He is currently serving a three year sentence for an intent to manufacture charge.

Scars That are Going to Leave a Mark

Melvin Miles

Most of my earliest memories are almost all negative. Let me elaborate. When I was about four years old, living in Gonzalez, Louisiana, we were having a coon-ass crawfish boil with all the fixings. Fifty pounds of crawfish, sausage, mushrooms, onions, etc...It was gonna be the shit. Everybody was there, mom, dad, my uncle Kenny, his wife and kids and a few of our closest neighbors.

All of us kids were horsing around and playing as kids will do. Then my cousin Rachel wanted me to swing her. This was back when the swings were built with the slide right by the swing so that two kids could sit facing two other kids while they swung back and forth. So I got on the slide and started swinging her back and forth. When I felt like it was going fast enough, I made my move and tried to jump onto the swing with her. My timing was just a bit off and the pivot point by the seat caught me just right and cut my dick clean off. So I fall to the ground and roll under the closest car and I ball into the fetal position, bleeding like a stuck pig screaming my head off. It took my mother and a couple others to get me out from under the car to be able to rush me to the hospital so the doctor could sew it back on. After the doctor sew it back on, he told me I could not go swimming 'till it healed and I get the stitches out. The no swimming had me almost as upset as the temporary amputation.

The next winter my Aunt Ursula bought me a silver bracelet that was set with turquoise. I was obsessed with this bracelet. I wouldn't take it off for nothing in the world, nobody could get me to take the damn thing off. I thought I would lose it if I did. Finally, one day my Aunt Ursula convinced me to take it off, that nobody would get it if I did. So I took it off and we left to go swimming down by the levee.

While we were gone to the levee to go swimming our house burnt to the ground with everything we owned, including my bracelet. This was the end of the world to me, I was devastated.

Things picked up and got better until close to my 8th birthday. This is when my grandpa, who I am named after, came down with lung cancer. Paw Paw Mel was our solid rock. This is one of the most amazing people I've ever known. He was a professional hockey player, boxer and he was a captain on tug boats among other things, but the thing that influenced me the most I believe was that he was a boat captain. This man for me was probably the only positive male role model in my life. He was bigger than life. But right before my 8th birthday, he died with cancer and this truly devastated me.

A couple years later my mother married one big mean son-of-a bitch who didn't tolerate me too much. He treated me like an indentured servant. He would make me work in the evenings after school sanding cabinets. On the holidays and summers, I would have to go to work with him at Pascagoula Sheet Metal cleaning the shop and sorting the scrap metal out into bins. When I worked at the sheet metal shop, I did get paid twenty-five cents an hour. But if I didn't do things to his specifications or slower than he wanted it done he would beat my ass with a 2X4 or the buckle of his cowboy belt buckle. One time while I was listening to him beat my mother's ass, I loaded my 20 gauge and stepped around the corner and leveled it at him, but as I pulled the hammer back the telephone rang and he stopped to answer the damn phone. I guess it's a good thing because from where I was I would have shot him in his back.

The next year during my summer, I can't say vacation because I was putting in my forty hours at the shop, but hey I had a raise, I was making fifty cents an hour, my mother came down with double pneumonia and they hospitalized her. Because she was doing so bad they put her into a drug induced coma to try to conserve her energy to help her recover from this illness. So my step-father decides maybe it would be best to send me to stay with my father down in Florida for a while. The day I arrived down in Florida my step monster pulled me to the side and told me "You remember all those nice Christmases you used to have?" I said, "Yes" she said, "Well they are fucking over with." I started school down in Florida and soon after my 13th birthday my mother died from complications due to the pneumonia.

So things rocked along with me doing my best to make her life a living hell and her reciprocating and making mine a living hell. She would cook shit I didn't like and try to make me sit at the table all night. One night, her mother was down from Virginia and we were eating some shit I didn't like but when she left the room her mother raked the shit onto her plate and leaned over and whispered in my ear "She's a bitch."

Well, they put up with me through one Christmas which she made sure was not what I wanted it to be. By the next Christmas, she'd put up with all she cared to put up with. She went to dear old dad and told him it's him or me! She was gonna leave if he didn't get rid of me. So on Christmas Eve, they gave me one suitcase and told me to put in it what I could and drove me to the bus station on the way to stay with my stepfather.

It's 1987 and I am fourteen years old. The fair has come to Pascagoula. The four of us Steve, Shawn, Mark, and myself are passing a booth and the carnie makes his pitch "Hey lost boys throw the ball win a prize!" This gets us to thinking and we decide this is what we will be known as, "The Lost Boys". We start hanging out at the point in Pascagoula. This is where we hang out, getting drunk, smoking dope, and chasing girls on the weekends. Word spreads and our little gang grows. The Crips take notice and take offense. Well they "The Crips" decide they want to beat our asses up. Well that doesn't set well with the Crips, Archie Bourgeois' nightmares, and a few other people I run with. Now we the Lost Boys, the bloods, the Nightmares, and a few others, decide we will all fight against the Crips and their people in the chow hall during lunch. The principal of our school, Moss Point High, has different plans, he calls me into his office. He informs me he knows what's going on and that he is gonna expel me for what he calls congregation.

I transfer to Alba High School in Bayou La Batre, AL. Unbeknownst to me one of the students at my new school is dating someone from my old school. The situation follows me to my new school with the added twist of Devil Worship rolled up into it for good measure. Things really start to spiral out of control now. Apparently the people in Bayou La Batre have a problem with Devil Worshipers and it starts to run in the papers and on the news.

One day the principal calls me to the office to talk about "stuff you could bring to school." He asks me what types of things could I bring to school that were not allowed. I tell him drugs, knives, all kinds of stuff. He says what about guns? And I say yes I guess so if I wanted to.

The next day my Aunt picks me up early so I can go to a concert and when she does the principal calls me into his office and tells me he is gonna throw me out for bringing a pistol to school the day before. He told me he had statements from six students stating I had a gun the day before on campus. I went to the juvenile division to discuss this with a juvey officer with my grandma. When the officer got up and went out for a minute, I had a chance to read the statement written by these six 15 year old students. I was amazed to see these six kids describe only two things about a gun. They all said it was a Ruger with a 3 ½ inch barrel. Now for six people to look at a gun and notice the barrel length, and type of gun for that matter, and none of them describing anything else, that would be a sheer miracle.

Along the time the principal threw me out for this fabricated gun, the Devil Worship accusations began to escalate. My grandma and two of her aunts go to a meeting about the Devil Worship problem. As she is sitting there in the back this meeting, it starts to heat up and this guy gets up and says what are we gonna do about this Melvin Miles? Grandma says about this time half the community center jumps up and says "Yes, what are we gonna do about him"? So she does the only prudent thing she could and slid the hell out of there before anyone recognized her.

Now, the whole town is talking about me and Devil Worship...It's on the news, in the newspapers, everything. About this time a guy a couple years younger than me who was involved in the aforementioned Devil Worship, by the name of Jeff Howard, kills himself. Within a couple of days, two detectives knock on our front door. I answer the door and kind of step back and one of them says, "We need to speak with Melvin Miles." I say, "Speaking". He says "Not you, we're looking for the older one." I say, "He's not here." As all this is going on my grandma has walked up behind me and she says "This is the only one we have what can we do for you?" These two detectives come in and inform us that they are investigating Mr. Howard's murder-suicide, and that according to their sources I was the leader of his cult and that I'm their prime suspect in his death. As the investigation rocks on with these detectives watching me come and go for months they finally realize it's all bullshit and after about six months they come to our house. They end up telling me that they knew I was not involved in the cult, did not know Jeff Howard, had never met him, but the detectives said that this investigation had cost the county $42,000 and they had followed the Devil Worshippers chain of command so high up that they had found people in Mobile's politics involved in this cult and even though I was not involved in anything per se but these people in politics they were talking about had a vendetta out for me and that I had no win in Mobile,

AL. And this is one of the first times I remember thinking damn I have got to be Hitler in his next reincarnation because nobody else could have amassed this big of a karmic debt.

Addendum: Evidence of a Successful Program

MSP Hosts the "Prison Writes Initiative"

Office of Communications

PARCHMAN - Writings of state inmates who completed the first class of the Mississippi Prison Writes Initiative could be published and released this fall.

The inmates spent 18 weeks learning the basic of poetry, fiction, and then memoir writing at the Mississippi Penitentiary at Parchman. They studied the works of a wide range of writers, including Mississippi natives Eudora Welty and Barry Hannah, Langston Hughes, Rita Dove, William Styron, Judith Tannenbaum, Wallace Stevens, Spoon Jackson and Margret Atwood.

Such classes have been shown to help reduce recidivism, said instructor Louis Bourgeois, executive director of an Oxford-based nonprofit that is a venue for both emerging and existing writers.

"Some of our best writers are coming out of prison these days," he said. "It's amazing."

The class, believed to be the first of its kind in the Mississippi Department of Corrections' system, far exceeded his expectations, Bourgeois said.

"The group I worked with were for the most part exceptional writers and students," he said. "The (Mississippi Humanities Council) evaluator who visited the class on May 5th, said it was the best class he ever observed. What I learned from the class was what I expected all along, that writing can change lives?"

Bourgeois brought the class to MSP with the support of the MHC after having taught at the University of Mississippi, Marshall County Correctional Facility, and Rust College and for the Mississippi Arts Commission. As a publisher interested in literature from marginalized groups, he said, "I'm a

Professor Louis Bourgeois, executive director of the Oxford-based nonprofit VOX Press, spent 18 weeks teaching inmates basic writing during the Prison Writes Initiative program at Parchman.

firm believer that all people in society should be educated no matter who they are."

Bourgeois said the setting fits perfectly with VOX PRESS, the nonprofit that Bourgeois cofounded in 2004. The class started with 15 students, most of whom had not obtained their GED, on Jan. 20 and ended June 2 with nine completing it.

Bourgeois said he didn't deal with controversial issues or let the inmates use their creative outlet to retry their cases. Rather, he stuck to his plan to endorse nothing other than creative writing.

"The point of the class is to cultivate a love of reading and writing," he said. "I really do think this community needs to be exposed to great writing."

He also accomplished his goal to end with a collection of publishable material. Most of the stories in the book will deal primarily with inmates early childhood memories, such as their first day of school or spending time at grandmother's house.

"In other states where creative programs have been established in state prisons, this is quite common," Bourgeois said. The book, once completed, is pending MDOC's approval.

"Any sales from the book will be used to support the Prison Writes Initiative," Bourgeois said.

Some eligible student inmates have been recommended to the commissioner for special Meritorious Earned Time (MET), which is offered to offenders for satisfactory participation in education and work programs. However, the MHC evaluator and Emmitt Sparkman, director of Education at MSP, noted students seemed to be inspired by simply being in the class.

"The MSP Education Department appreciates Professor Bourgeois offering a creative writing course to the offenders,' Sparkman said. "The participants seem to genuinely enjoy the experience."

The plan is to offer another session of Prison Writes Initiative this fall at Parchman.

"The MHC would do a lot of good if it were to repeat such program or to expand upon them," said Eric Weber, an associate professor in the Department of Public Policy Leadership at the University of Mississippi, in his evaluation of the program.

Weber said he found the inmates' stories not only fascinating "but their works are artful and clearly inspired by the instruction they received from Mr. Bourgeois. The program was both highly important and remarkably well run, an excellent use of MHC funds."■

"Mississippi Prison Writes" at Parchman Prison

Errol Castens - Associated Press - Friday, June 13 2014

as seen on WashingtonTimes.com

PARCHMAN, Miss. (AP) - Picture students in a classroom, poring for weeks over Spoon Jackson, Eudora Welty, Langston Hughes and others.

Later, armed with new perspectives from such masters, the students create their own words, mining their own experiences and feelings for nuggets of insight and truth.

The class might be at most any college in America, except students' clothing signifies not school pride but security status, and their campus is surrounded by razor wire.

This is "Mississippi Prison Writes." This is Parchman penitentiary.

About a dozen inmates spent the spring semester under the tutelage of writer and publisher Louis Bourgeois. The program emerged from the mission of the nonprofit he heads, Vox Press, to support efforts to give voice to marginalized artists.

"Some of our greatest writers and artists may very well be housed in Mississippi's oldest and largest prison, Parchman Farm," he said at a June 2 graduation ceremony.

Teaching the five-month class has done nothing to dampen that outlook.

"Their awareness was heightened by the exercise of writing, because none of them had ever written before in this particular way," Bourgeois said.

Nathaniel Murphree works with the Adult Basic Education program at Parchman and has been a liaison with the Mississippi Prison Writes program.

"This is the first time we've done this," he said.

While many students are seeking general equivalency diplomas (GEDs), this class was designed for a different kind of student. From high school dropouts to those with college experience, all came equipped with a craving to learn.

"We had to find the folks that we thought would be most interested," Murphree said.

Bourgeois said students' writings helped him see more clearly how they ended up in prison.
"They came up with some fairly rich accounts about their mostly impoverished childhoods," he said. "You're seeing how they eventually got into trouble from the way they grew up. There's a lot of self-awareness in their writing.

"There seems to have been a brutal honesty."

Selected writings from the class are aimed for publication as a limited-release volume, "In Our Own Words," by Vox Press.

On the last day of class, students read excerpts from their memoirs.

One black man related his first day in school in the 1960s, where he was around white children for the first time and wondered why many avoided him. For good and bad, he said, school opened "a new world that would change me forever."

Another described a childhood home where poverty and hunger and chaos were interrupted only by occasional visits to his grandmother, whose cooking and compassion seemed almost magical.

At home, he said, "The only thing that seemed to change was the days of the week. Christmas was something that didn't happen for us."

One inmate recalled catching a ride with a policeman at age 9, when a downpour threatened his armload of library books.

"There would be many more such rides in my life none of them with so happy an ending," he said.

Mississippi Prison Writes is sponsored by the Mississippi Humanities Council, the Fedder Foundation, Neil White, Carol Dorsey and the Cox Foundation.

———
Information from: Northeast Mississippi Daily Journal, http://djournal.com

"My Experience   5-12-14
in the MS Prison Writes Class - Spring 2014 "
— S.K. Shaddix, #179638

— This class has been the high point of my
week here in Parchman.   I've been able
to find my motivation to spend at least
an hour everyday writing. Often it will
be longer, but it has become a big part
of my mornings and sometimes my evenings.

— The structure of the class, with its weekly
assignments of topics to write on, and
hand-outs to read create a disciplined
routine that makes it effective.

— My classmates were hesitant at first,
to join in a discussion over the stories
we've read over the week, but early on that
changed. I remember that day well, because
it was like a spark. Suddenly everyone was
pitching into the mix their viewpoints, thoughts,
and ideas. Hubbub is a good description for it.

— Mr. Bourgeois has brought to us a gift, thank
you to him, and everyone else who has made this
possible. Please let it continue.
                                    SK.Shaddix

How do I feel about the prison) Vincent Young #37525
writing class initiative   Unit-30-C
This class has open up a lot for   Parchman MS
me. It gives me the chance to   38738
write about my life. I've been in prison for
24 yrs and I have a daughter that is 27 years old.
She has a 8 year old daughter. I am truly bless
by God to have them in my life. This writing
class have giving me the chance to express to
my daughter and grandchild how I grew up.
It gives them not only my love but also my
heart. I never knew I could write or bad
away with words. But truly this class have
giving me freedom. Freedom to express to
the world that I am human. That I have
a heart that I love just like everyone else.
I will ~~always~~ always be thankful for this class
cause it has giving me a new world to enter.
Once this class is over I will continue to
write. Not only for myself but also for my
grandchild.

Participant Experience

Seriell Belton #33571
Unit 30
Parchman MS. 38738

May 12, 2014

I'm Seriell Belton and presently a
inmate here at Parchman Prison. I'm writing
to those who might be concerned, curious, or
that just really care. I would like to give my
views, feelings and true thoughts concerning the
prison writes class that's offered here at
parchman by Mr. Professor Louis Bourgeois.

First of all I want to thank Mr.
Professor Louis Bourgeois for the warm thought
and caring spirit for even considering the
forgotten and down trotted men that resides
here temporarily and some even for their entire
lives.

This class that Professor Bourgeois
offers has opened up for me and have given me
a desire to write, and a outlet of expression, which
I truly value and thank Professor Bourgeois for.

My prayer and hope is that this program
will continue, exspand, and produce great
writers for many years to come.

Sincerly
Seriell Belton

Participant Experience

Clifton Nichols

How do I feel about the Prison Writes Initiative?

When I first heard about the creative writing class being offered at Unit 30, I was somewhat apprehensive about joining it. I was already fairly busy teaching and tutoring literary on the zone and in the (ABE) school. However, by the time I decided to join all the fifthteen students had been chosen. It was a month later that the administrator Mr. Murphree would meet with me and ask that I be in the school. It seems as some students had dropped out and there were openings to be filled. I reluctantly agreed to attend and the only reserve being that I would be a month behind everyone else.

I attended my first class, met the other students, met Mr. Bourgeois, the instructor, recieved instructions for what and how to write and took off. I eagerly and passionately approached the writing about my life and automatically wrote 20 pages the first week. It stimulated my mental process in such a way as nothing else had in so long, A long needed in-road and outlet for my life's feelings. I was at the least feeling exhuberant and lively as my mind danced in all moments of the day about personal subject matter. A great RELEASE!

This would only be accentuated by the Monday afternoon classes with the additional readings of other authors and the reading with our own writings, which would be critiqued by the other class members. This was not at the least to say an exhilirating experience for me to hear first

How do I Feel about the Prison writing class iNitiative?
The Prison writing class has been Very helpful to me.
I've learned better ways to express myself Via
writing essays. My Vocabulary has also improved
greatly because of the extensive amount of
writing. I Feel a sense of Joy to be a part of
the writing class.
Mr Louis E. Bourgeois is an excellent writing
instructor. He gives us work assignmets to enhance
our creative writing potential.

EARNEST HERRING #41881

1. I have always love writing.
2. The creative writing program provided a format for me to be able to write and learn about writing.
3. It exposed me to different type of writers and their literary works.
4. Also Mr. Louis Bourgeois is a great motivator as well as a great instructor.
5. I encourage anyone interested in the art of writing to take the class.
6. I also love the setting of the class.
7. It's unlike any other setting in prison, because it allows the inmates to engage in deep discussions about their work. These discussions are done on an intellectual level in which the inmates can disagree without it turning into a violent confrontation.
8. Hell! maybe Mr. Bourgeois should become the warden.

by: #37
5-12-14
MSP # 144000 Gregory Frazier

Participant Experience

By. Melvin Miles
185678

How I feel about this prison writes Class. The class Mr. Bourgeious has started teaching here at Parchman has been the most liberating classes I have ever been thru. It has helped in being able to express my self in ways I did not believe possible. It helped me to understand a side of me that I never even wanted to face, much less put down on paper. Before this class I would not express myself on paper because because I always felt like I would look stupid but since taking this class I now know I can express myself on paper without looking like a complete idiot.

I am greatful to Mr. Bourgeious for all he has done in bringing us this class. I appreciate the chance to have taken this class + would love to attend any other classes he brings here + gives me the opportunity to take. This class has been a breath of fresh air in a place stale with the oppression and tyrany of prison politic's. Thank you Mr. Bourgeios for your time + dilligent teaching. Keep up the good work. This place needs more people like you.

Participant Experience

HARRY BOSTICK #156660

How I Feel About the Prison Rights Initiative

I have been Attending A creative writing class at the Mississippi State Penitentiary in Parchman, Mississippi. The class started in January of 2014 and will end the last week of May, 2014. It is a weekly class and the instructor is MR. Louis Bourgoise.

I have thoroughly enjoyed this creative writing class. It has given me some exposure to various types and kinds of writings. The class as a whole seemed to gravitate toward memoir writing. Simply put, we all have a story to tell and MR. Bourgoise has shown us how to present our stories in written form. He has critiqued our work and allowed us to critique others work, which has greatly improved my writing ability. I look forward to the class each week and it gives me something positive to work on between classes.

I appreciate MR. Bourgoise taking his time to bring A little light to A very DARK PLACE.

Participant Experience

Prison Writes Class Course Evaluation
Professor Louis Bourgeois
MSP Training Building

S.K. Shaddix
6-2-14

(left margin, handwritten vertical) ⊛ Referral: Eric Potts, #155075, 39/c-B/165, Renew: Jr. Kerry Shaddix, 179638, 30/a-B/184

- ① What were the best aspects of this course and the instructor? ② How was the course helpful? Please be specific.

① motivation provided for me to write every day.
② driven to have one story to turn in each week.

- ① Do you believe your writing and reading skills have improved? If so, how did the course promote this improvement? ② Do you feel you will be able to sustain a writing and reading discipline once you leave the class?

① yes, especially with the provided dictionary
② I do, because even through the holiday breaks, I've
   continued to write early in the morning, on a daily basis

- ① Were the instructor's written and oral comments on your pieces helpful? ② Were in-class writing and reading exercises useful and stimulating?

① They were, yes.
② The in-class discussions were high energy!

- ① How has your own attitude toward writing changed because you took this course? ② Do you feel more or less interested in writing and reading? ③ Do you feel this course helped you better understand the difficulties and pitfalls as well as the techniques of writing? Be specific.

① I've become more serious about my writing
② more
③ yes   the stories each person did

- After taking this course, what do you consider to be your greatest strengths as a writer—and your greatest weaknesses?

very good at dialogue, titles, concepts, and beginnings

※ constant challenge to complete stories that I've started.

— This workshop gave me the structure I needed to flourish. A deadline: "Finish this by Monday." Please replay this for those like me.

I go home 9-28-14, Sun.

111

Participant Evaluation

Prison Writes Class Course Evaluation
Professor Louis Bourgeois
MSP Training Building

- What were the best aspects of this course and the instructor? How was
  the course helpful? Please be specific.

  I NOW Know how to white My Memoir
  Thank you

- Do you believe your writing and reading skills have improved? If so, how *yes*
  did the course promote this improvement? Do you feel you will be able to
  sustain a writing and reading discipline once you leave the class?

  Yes, my whiting skills have improved And I Am very
  Appreciative to MR. Bourgeois for teaching to class
  yes, I cAn will sustain my whiting.

- Were the instructor's written and oral comments on your pieces helpful?
  Were in-class writing and reading exercises useful and stimulating?

  The instructors written And oral comments were A highlight
  of the class. The readings + whitings were very useful +
  stimulating

- How has your own attitude toward writing changed because you took this
  course? Do you feel more or less interested in writing and reading? Do
  you feel this course helped you better understand the difficulties and
  pitfalls as well as the techniques of writing? Be specific.

  I Appreciate And respect AN Author more than I Did
  I Am more interested in whiting Now.
  Yes, the difficulties of And techiques of whiting Are Alot
  more understandable Now

- After taking this course, what do you consider to be your greatest
  strengths as a writer—and your greatest weaknesses?

  whiting Memoir's.

112

Participant Evaluation

Clifton Nickens

Prison Writes Class Course Evaluation
Professor Louis Bourgeois
MSP Training Building

- What were the best aspects of this course and the instructor? How was the course helpful? Please be specific. MR. Bourgeois was great in his knowledge and experience of memoir writing. It has greatly improved my writing ability.

- Do you believe your writing and reading skills have improved? If so, how did the course promote this improvement? Do you feel you will be able to sustain a writing and reading discipline once you leave the class? yes, much improved. By the exercise of mental recall, usage of words to express ideas. Yes, I have already begun to write more.

- Were the instructor's written and oral comments on your pieces helpful? Were in-class writing and reading exercises useful and stimulating? The instructor was always fair and unbiased. The class workshops of critiquing each other's writing was very helpful.

- How has your own attitude toward writing changed because you took this course? Do you feel more or less interested in writing and reading? Do you feel this course helped you better understand the difficulties and pitfalls as well as the techniques of writing? Be specific. Yes, it takes much discipline and skill to be a successful writer.

- After taking this course, what do you consider to be your greatest strengths as a writer—and your greatest weaknesses? My strength is in my ability to be descriptive. My weakness is my wordiness or inability to express my ideas concisely.

113

Participant Evaluation

Prison Writes Class Course Evaluation
Professor Louis Bourgeois
MSP Training Building

- What were the best aspects of this course and the instructor? How was the course helpful? Please be specific. I didn't know I could be a writer. ~~xxxx~~ until I took this class. The instructor boost my spirit on writing

- Do you believe your writing and reading skills have improved? If so, how did the course promote this improvement? Do you feel you will be able to sustain a writing and reading discipline once you leave the class? YES

- Were the instructor's written and oral comments on your pieces helpful? Were in-class writing and reading exercises useful and stimulating? yes the instructor was very helpful

- How has your own attitude toward writing changed because you took this course? Do you feel more or less interested in writing and reading? Do you feel this course helped you better understand the difficulties and pitfalls as well as the techniques of writing? Be specific. I believe in myself I will continue to write.

- After taking this course, what do you consider to be your greatest strengths as a writer—and your greatest weaknesses? How to express myself threw words

Vincent Young #37525

Participant Evaluation

Prison Writes Class Course Evaluation
Professor Louis Bourgeois
MSP Training Building

- What were the best aspects of this course and the instructor? How was the course helpful? Please be specific.

  The writing improved my writing ability.

- Do you believe your writing and reading skills have improved? If so, how did the course promote this improvement? Do you feel you will be able to sustain a writing and reading discipline once you leave the class? yes.

- Were the instructor's written and oral comments on your pieces helpful? Were in-class writing and reading exercises useful and stimulating?

  Yes, the instructor was very helpful.
  Yes, the writing was also very stimulating.

- How has your own attitude toward writing changed because you took this course? Do you feel more or less interested in writing and reading? Do you feel this course helped you better understand the difficulties and pitfalls as well as the techniques of writing? Be specific.

  The writing course was a plus.

- After taking this course, what do you consider to be your greatest strengths as a writer—and your greatest weaknesses?

  My greatest strengths is long writing.
  My greatest weakness was writing about childhood.

  Earnest Herring 4/88

Letters of Reccommendation

Neil White

April 29, 2014

Dear Students of the Prison Writes Initiative,

I'm so sorry I can't be there, in person, to speak to all of you.

I admire that you're exploring the written word. As you probably understand, the best stories are filled with conflict, angst, drama and obstacles. Those of us who have been through the criminal justice system never lack for that kind of material. In many ways, it is the best thing that can happen to a writer.

In 1999, I was at a writers conference in Sewanee, Tennessee. During one of the evening social events, I stood in the corner of the room wearing a buttondown shirt, blue blazer, and khaki pants. Two women writers from New York — both wearing long scarves, denim dresses, and boots — approached me. I could tell the didn't think someone dressed in traditional college-boy attire would have anything important to write.

"You were in a fraternity, weren't you?" the taller woman asked me.

"Yes," I said. "In fact, I was president of my fraternity."

They both smirked.

"What do you have to write about?" the other woman asked.

"Well," I said, "I was in federal prison with the last victims of leprosy in America."

In unison they both said, "You're so lucky!!"

I recount this story to illustrate the gift you've been given. Very few writers have seen the side of life you've experienced. Most would kill to get to know the characters who occupy your world.

What's bad for your life is good for your writing. I trust you will put the experience to good use.

I look forward to reading — and endorsing — your work.

With gratitude,

Neil White
Author, *In the Sanctuary of Outcasts*

Letters of Reccommendation

May 23, 2014

To Whom it May Concern:

This past April, I was fortunate to visit the writing class Louis Bourgeois launched at Parchman Farm. In addition to the class visit itself, in the few days of my visit, Louis and I continued a conversation we'd begun over email about teaching in prison. I write in strong support of what Louis is doing now and strong support, as well, for his vision of more extensive arts programming in Mississippi prisons.

Louis asked me to visit because I was a California Arts Council Artist-in-Residence sharing poetry at San Quentin from 1985-1989. I also wrote *A Manual for Artists Working in Prison* for Arts-in-Corrections (California's prison arts program for close to thirty years), did a feasibility study for arts programming in Minnesota prisons in the early '90s, wrote two published memoirs about the work at San Quentin, visited prisons and arts programs in many states as a guest artist and as a panel and keynote speaker, and am part of an informal national group of prison arts colleagues.

As I write, my own work inside California prisons was part of a statewide prison arts program. The other states I've visited have also had programs (some through universities, some through nonprofits, some through church groups). Louis is doing his work through Vox Press, but there's no existing prison arts programming – no existing programming of any kind, as I understand it – at Parchman or elsewhere in Mississippi prisons. Louis intends to both continue the class he's offered for five months and to expand on what he's begun and I urge you to support him.

I urge this support both in general – I've seen the value of prison arts programs for decades – and in particular: Louis is doing excellent work. Arts programming is valuable from the prison's and state's point of view as it has been shown to reduce both negative incidents inside and also to lower the recidivism rate for participants. California's Brewster Report documents these benefits. In less formal documentation, it's clear from experience that the men and woman in prison who are able to participate in arts classes have a space – a classroom and an invitation – to create from what's best in themselves; to call on memory, observation, and imagination to make something new and beautiful; to develop skills to shape what they create as well as possible; to exert the discipline required to make what they make; to share with each other in an atmosphere of support and safety; and to give back something positive to the outside world.

Louis's students in particular are working on long prose which – as I well know having written books myself – demands commitment, discipline, and the willingness to struggle against and prevail over one's own demons. The bulk of the writing these men do is in their cells, on their own time. The class is a place to share and receive feedback, but they're individually responsible for getting the writing done. Unlike any other prison arts program I've seen, Louis began his class with the intention to publish his students' work. Vox Press can do that. For any writer, the knowledge that your work will be published – shared with an audience – is a powerful motivation. Knowing others will read your words makes you responsible to your

Further Evaluation

Grant # RG13-11-090

"Prison Writes Program"
Yoknapatawpha Arts Council
413 South 14th Street
Oxford, MS 38655
Spring 2014

Grant Evaluation Report

5/6/14

Cover sheet

This report offers an evaluation of the "Prison Writes Program," delivered in Parchman Prison. The program was profoundly meaningful to the inmates. They said that they had never really written before the class, yet they were writing 15-25 page narratives about their lives. Not only were their stories fascinating, but their works are artful and clearly inspired by the instruction they received from Mr. Bourgeois. The program was both highly important and remarkably well run, an excellent use of MHC funds. The MHC would do a lot of good if it were to repeat such program or to expand upon them.

Evaluator:

Dr. Eric Thomas Weber
Associate Professor
Department of Public Policy Leadership
The University of Mississippi
105 Odom Hall
University, MS 38677
Phone: 662.915.1336
Fax: 662.915.1954
Email: etweber@olemiss.edu
Web site: EricThomasWeber.org

The University of Mississippi

Oxford • Jackson • Tupelo • Southaven

Department of Public Policy Leadership
Post Office Box 175
University, MS 38677-0175
(662) 915-7347
Fax: (662) 915-1954

June 23, 2014

Re: Louis Bourgeois and his course delivered at Parchman Prison

To whom it may concern,

I am writing to serve as a reference for Louis Bourgeois and the course that he delivered on memoir-writing at Parchman Prison in 2014. I am associate professor of Public Policy Leadership at the University of Mississippi, with a background in moral and political philosophy. I served as an external evaluator for a Mississippi Humanities Council grant which supported Louis's course at the prison. I am writing now independently of the state humanities council to let others know about the remarkable interactions I had the pleasure of witnessing between Louis and the student-prisoners at Parchman Prison.

Prior to attending a meeting of Louis's course on memoir-writing at Parchman Prison, I had not known him or Vox, the non-profit recipient of the grant. The long trip from Oxford to Parchman alone was evidence of Louis's enthusiasm and his wish to offer educational opportunities to all citizens, including those in prison. I only made the one round-trip visit, but Louis made the long drive weekly for the duration of the course and grant period. On the drive I enjoyed getting to know him, but it was in the classroom that I was most taken with his abilities as a humanities scholar and artist. Louis was professional, prepared, and early. We arrived in time to ensure that he had a chance to talk with the prison's director of education. It was clear from the staff at the prison that courses like the one Louis offered are welcome and desired, but that such opportunities are few. The students in Louis's class made the matter especially clear: they were deeply grateful for his course.

After taking care of preliminaries, such as copies for handouts, Louis joined the inmates who were all seated in the classroom, eagerly organizing their stacks of writing. Each was enthusiastically ready to submit stories, their own memoirs, to Louis, myself, and anyone interested in reading them. In good pedagogical fashion, Louis began the class with an exercise of reading over a text that everyone had in handout form, which featured excellent and artful prose. As a person who has taught for around a dozen years, I can tell you that it takes some thoughtful selection and preparation to pick a text read together which evokes student responses and rich interactions. I was profoundly impressed with the

Further Evaluation

prisoners' eagerness to jump in and discuss the material, to raise questions, and generally to interact seriously in discussion.

I have witnessed many classes taught by others. In each instance, the students felt somewhat self-conscious, given the presence of a guest observer. The only way I noted the inmates' reactions, however, was in their insistence that I appreciate how much the course meant to them. It was clear that, for many of them, this course was their first exposure to advanced intellectual engagement of this kind. They were hungry for the interactions. Every time a text was to be read, a student was ready to jump into reading the material aloud. I felt a certain amount of envy – desire to work with students so intensely interested in and grateful for the course. There was no hint that any of the students took the opportunity for granted. In addition, it was clearly a valued outlet for students' frustrations, feelings, and desire to be heard.

I was most moved when the students read their own work aloud. The range was remarkable, with some students writing about the treatment they had experienced in the penal system to others who wrote about their childhood. I remember one prisoner-student who wrote about what Christmas was like growing up in a family that could not do anything special for the holidays, though everyone else he knew was celebrating and excited. His depictions of growing up in poverty were moving and powerful. Another author wrote a beautiful depiction of going through forced school integration. He was too uncomfortable to read it himself, so one of his peers stepped in and was willing to read it to the class for him. The piece described the colors the author saw at school with reference to a box of crayons thrown open. Though my visit was months ago now, I still remember his reference to the intense commotion of joining a large school, with people going quickly in all directions, like a knocked-over ant hill. His language was elegant and his imagery was striking. I cannot do his work justice in my description from memory. Nevertheless, I can tell you that I have very few times in my educational and teaching career been as moved by student-teacher interactions as I was on my visit to Parchman Prison.

The matter that was clearest in my experience visiting Parchman and Louis's class was that more opportunities like the one he offered are wanted and needed. Some of the students told me that they felt transformed by the experience. If in any way you can encourage or support Louis's and Vox's efforts to deliver programming like what I witnessed at Parchman Prison, I strongly recommend that you do it.

If you have any questions for me about Louis, feel free to call me at 662.915.1336 or email me at etweber@olemiss.edu.

Sincerely,

Eric Weber

Eric Thomas Weber, Ph.D.
Associate Professor
http://EricThomasWeber.org

PARCHMAN VOCATIONAL SCHOOL

CERTIFICATE OF COMPLETION

Clifton Nickens

HAS SUCCESFULLY COMPLETED ALL REQUIREMENTS OF THE PRISON WRITES INITIATIVE FOR THE SPRING 2014 TERM AT THE PARCHMAN VOCATIONAL SCHOOL, ON THIS DAY JUNE 2, 2014.

_____
Academic Instructor

_____
Program Director

PARCHMAN VOCATIONAL SCHOOL

CERTIFICATE OF COMPLETION

Ernest Herring

HAS SUCCESFULLY COMPLETED ALL REQUIREMENTS OF THE PRISON WRITES INITIATIVE FOR THE SPRING 2014 TERM AT THE PARCHMAN VOCATIONAL SCHOOL, ON THIS DAY JUNE 2, 2014.

_____   _____
Academic Instructor   *Program Director*

PARCHMAN VOCATIONAL SCHOOL

CERTIFICATE OF COMPLETION

Gregory Frazier

HAS SUCCESFULLY COMPLETED ALL REQUIREMENTS OF THE PRISON WRITES INITIATIVE FOR THE SPRING 2014 TERM AT THE PARCHMAN VOCATIONAL SCHOOL, ON THIS DAY JUNE 2, 2014.

_____
Academic Instructor

_____
Program Director

PARCHMAN VOCATIONAL SCHOOL

CERTIFICATE OF COMPLETION

Melvin Miles

HAS SUCCESFULLY COMPLETED ALL REQUIREMENTS OF THE PRISON WRITES INITIATIVE FOR THE SPRING 2014 TERM AT THE PARCHMAN VOCATIONAL SCHOOL, ON THIS DAY JUNE 2, 2014.

_____   _____
Academic Instructor   *Program Director*

PARCHMAN VOCATIONAL SCHOOL

CERTIFICATE OF COMPLETION

Seriehel Belton

HAS SUCCESFULLY COMPLETED ALL REQUIREMENTS OF THE PRISON WRITES INITIATIVE FOR THE SPRING 2014 TERM AT THE PARCHMAN VOCATIONAL SCHOOL, ON THIS DAY JUNE 2, 2014.

_____
Academic Instructor

_____
Program Director

PARCHMAN VOCATIONAL SCHOOL

CERTIFICATE OF COMPLETION

Harry Bostick

HAS SUCCEFULLY COMPLETED ALL REQUIREMENTS OF THE PRISON
WRITES INITIATIVE FOR THE SPRING 2014 TERM AT THE PARCHMAN
VOCATIONAL SCHOOL, ON THIS DAY JUNE 2, 2014.

_____   _____
Academic Instructor   *Program Director*

PARCHMAN VOCATIONAL SCHOOL

CERTIFICATE OF COMPLETION

Steven Shaddix

HAS SUCCESFULLY COMPLETED ALL REQUIREMENTS OF THE PRISON WRITES INITIATIVE FOR THE SPRING 2014 TERM AT THE PARCHMAN VOCATIONAL SCHOOL, ON THIS DAY JUNE 2, 2014.

_____
Academic Instructor

_____
Program Director

PARCHMAN VOCATIONAL SCHOOL

CERTIFICATE OF COMPLETION

Vincent Young

HAS SUCCESFULLY COMPLETED ALL REQUIREMENTS OF THE PRISON WRITES INITIATIVE FOR THE SPRING 2014 TERM AT THE PARCHMAN VOCATIONAL SCHOOL, ON THIS DAY JUNE 2, 2014.

_____
Academic Instructor

_____
Program Director

About The Editor

Louis Bourgeois lives, writes, and edits in Oxford, Mississippi. The author of several books of poetry and prose, his memoir, The Gar Diaries, was nominated for the National Book Award in 2008. Bourgeois currently serves as the Executive Director of VOX PRESS, a 501 (c) 3 arts organization established to give marginalized individuals and groups a voice in the arts. Bourgeois also serves as an instructor for VOX 's Prison Writes Initiative (PWI), a writing and arts program for Mississippi inmates.

About Vox Press

VOX PRESS is a 501 (c) 3 arts organization based in Oxford, Mississippi. Its sole purpose of existence is to publish, perform, and disseminate the greatest works of art our age has to offer.

Please visit our website at www.voxpress.org